Living with Hope

Living with Hope
African Churches and HIV/AIDS 1

Ezra Chitando

WCC Publications, Geneva

Cover design: Marie Arnaud Snakkers

ISBN 978-2-8254-1523-8

© 2007, WCC Publications, World Council of Churches
P.O. Box 2100, 150 route de Ferney
1211 Geneva 2, Switzerland

Website: http://www.oikoumene.org/

External Copyright Permissions Requested

No. 119 in the Risk Book Series

Printed in France by IRL

Contents

Acknowledgements

The author wishes to express his deepest gratitude to many people who provided invaluable support in the writing of this book. Colleagues in the Ecumenical HIV/AIDS Initiative in Africa (EHAIA) – Nyambura Njoroge, Sue Parry, Charles Klagba, Jacinta Maingi, Ayoko Bahun-Wilson and Hendrew Lusey – provided information on the activities of churches in various parts of Africa. Christoph Mann and Musa Dube generously shared their insights on the meaning of AIDS competent churches and their experiences in EHAIA. Christine Chapwanya worked enthusiastically on the draft. The book benefited immensely from the Working Group on AIDS Competent Churches that met at the Ecumenical Institute, Bossey, Geneva, Switzerland from 23–27 July 2007. I thank Anna, Mutsawashe and Tinevimbo Chitando for their support.

This book is the first of a two-part series which deals with the African churches and HIV/AIDS. The second part, *Acting in Hope: African Churches and HIV/AIDS 2*, is also published as a Risk Book.

Introduction

Although research indicates that HIV/AIDS had occurred earlier in Africa,[1] it was only in the 1980s that most African governments acknowledged it. African nationalist rhetoric could not be reconciled easily with the stereotype of a diseased and dying continent. Governments feared the admission would prejudice tourism. Publications defended African integrity by means of conspiracy theories claiming that HIV and AIDS were the result of a plot by 'outsiders' to eliminate blacks.[2]

During this early phase, casual and dismissive attitudes towards HIV and AIDS predominated in most parts of Africa. The interpretation of AIDS as an 'American Idea to Discourage Sex' encapsulates such attitudes. HIV appeared remote and far-removed from African realities. Most African communities chose to focus on more pressing existential needs. Little did they know that the visitor who had pitched a tent in their midst was highly destructive and intended to stay.

Within a short time, HIV had become Africa's worst nightmare. By the mid-1990s, many communities had suffered from its disastrous effects:

> In the most affected regions, hard-earned improvements in health over the last 50 years have been overwhelmed by death and disability from AIDS. The disease is crippling progress at the personal, family, community and national levels. In severely affected nations, economic growth and political stability are also threatened.[3]

African politicians, artists, community leaders and others failed to realize that HIV and AIDS would completely transform the African landscape. After waging bitter struggles against colonialism, HIV and AIDS forced Africans to 'get

---

[1] Helen Jackson, *AIDS Africa: A Continent in Crisis*, Harare, SAFAIDS, 2002.

[2] For example, Richard C. Chirimuuta and Rosalind J. Chirimuuta, *Aids, Africa and Racism*, London, Richard Chirimuuta, 1987.

[3] Peter R. Lamptey, Jami L. Johnson and Marya Khan, 'The Global Challenge of HIV and AIDS', *Population Bulletin* 61, 2006, p. 3.

back on the road again'[4] and embark on another struggle with suffering and death. Resources mobilized for development were now needed to provide an effective response to HIV and AIDS.

The church in Africa found itself heavily implicated in this struggle. In its early phase, churches were keen to present the epidemic as a form of divine punishment to an apostate generation. Preachers claimed that the epidemic represented the 'signs of end times'. But with the passage of time, churches began to interrogate their responses to the epidemic. Critics and supporters of the church have continued to maintain that it has a major role to play in mitigating and ultimately eradicating HIV and AIDS. To understand this, we need to appreciate the history of the church in Africa.

Among the Shona people of Zimbabwe, as with other African cultural groups, visitors are to be treated with utmost courtesy. When visitors announce their departure, hosts are expected to try to persuade them to stay. When visitors leave, hosts are expected to see them out of the homestead. More importantly, they are also expected to travel with them for a good part of the journey. *Kuperekedza* (to accompany) implies identifying with the person undertaking a journey. In effect, they are told, 'You are not alone on this journey. I share your struggle.'[5]

The church in Africa is called upon to live out the positive attitude towards travellers that is found in African societies. It must express solidarity with people living with HIV. It must engage in *accompaniment*. It must travel with people living with HIV and be sensitive to their rights and needs. Crucially, it must break down barriers between 'us' and 'them'. A church 'with friendly feet' walks alongside those affected by HIV. It courageously proclaims that it is

---

[4] This evokes the title of a collection of poems by Freedom Nyamubaya, *On the Road Again*, Harare, Zimbabwe Publishing House, 1986.

[5] I am indebted to Manoj Kurian for enabling me to clarify this concept during a midnight discussion on accompaniment in Toronto, Canada, on 12 August 2006.

a church living with HIV and AIDS.[6] It refuses to throw stones (John 8:1–11) and recognizes that the gospel compels Christians to love without limits.

As it accompanies people and communities living with HIV and AIDS on journeys of faith,[7] the church with friendly feet ministers to every need. It repents of its negative attitudes, as well as the stigma and discrimination surrounding the disease. As it works with and among those living with HIV, it interrogates its theology, its attitude to sexuality and its gender insensitivity. It awakens to the realization that it must become an all-embracing community. A church with friendly feet does not pose questions about the moral standing of those with whom it is journeying.

---

[6] Donald Messer, *Breaking the Conspiracy of Silence: Christian Churches and the Global AIDS Crisis*, Minneapolis, Fortress Press, 2004, p. 28.

[7] See Gideon Byamugisha, Lucy Y. Steinitz, Glen Williams and Phumzile Zondi, *Journeys of Faith: Church-Based Responses to HIV and AIDS in Three Southern African Countries*, St Albans, TALC, 2002.

Chapter 1
The Church in Africa: An Overview

Today, there is a growing realization that Christianity's centre of gravity has shifted to Africa.[8] If we wish to make sense of the global Christian response to the epidemic, we need to analyse the reaction of the church in Africa. How the church in Africa has responded to HIV and AIDS provides a very strong indication of the overall Christian response to the epidemic.

Africa is a vast continent, with diverse cultures, histories and experiences. Hasty generalizations about it are often misleading. The church in Africa is equally characterized by diversity, with various modes of expression. Alongside the 'mainstream' or 'mainline' Protestant and Catholic churches, African Independent/Indigenous/Instituted/Initiated (AICs) and Pentecostal churches have a significant presence.[9] Each one of these forms of Christian expression has had its own experiences in relation to HIV and AIDS. And there are often differences between various dioceses within the same country.

Despite such national and local differences, and different theological traditions, we can still speak of the church in Africa. At one level, this is the result of a theological position that seeks to uphold unity in diversity. At another level, there exist similarities of response to HIV and AIDS across the denominations. Initially, the various denominations reacted to the epidemic with panic and condemnation. However, as time has gone by, many denominations in Africa have begun to strive to become AIDS competent. This book uses both the singular 'church' and the plural 'churches', signifying the theological aspiration for the unity of the body of Christ, while capturing the sociological and historical fact of pluralism within African Christianity.

What is the significance of the church in Africa? What distinctive characteristics does it bring to its overall response to HIV and AIDS?

---

[8] See Klaus Koschorke, 'Introduction', in Klaus Koschorke, ed., *African Identities and World Christianity in the Twentieth Century*, Wiesbaden, Harrassowitz, 2005, p. 9.

[9] Ezra Chitando, 'Naming the Phenomena: The Challenge of African Independent Churches', *Studia Historiae Ecclesiasticae* 31, 2005, pp. 85–110.

The church in Africa is undoubtedly a significant presence in the spiritual, social, political and economic lives of the people. It is thus strategically placed to make a difference in contexts of HIV and AIDS. However, in many ways, the church can be described as a 'sleeping giant'. When the church in Africa becomes fully AIDS competent, the effects of the epidemic will be significantly reduced.

Close cooperation (on the whole) between missionaries and colonialists in many parts of Africa created valuable church institutions such as schools, hospitals and universities.[10] In many countries, the church compliments the state in the provision of social services. Ownership of such institutions has given the church a voice in the politics of Africa.[11] Church leaders are often well placed to interact with politicians. In some instances this has led to the co-option of church leaders and a silencing of the prophetic voice but it also implies that influence can be brought to bear to effect positive change.

The church's investment in education has meant that a significant number of African political leaders received their education at mission schools. In the 1950s and 1960s, there was a close connection between Christianity and African nationalism.[12] Some political leaders are affiliated to specific denominations. The church is challenged to call these leaders to account when their policies hinder efforts to prevent the spread of HIV. It also has to be wary of politicians who seek to gain mileage out of their Christian identity. As a social institution located in a specific place and time,[13] the church in Africa enjoys a comparative advantage over secular non-governmental organizations (NGOs) that

---

[10] The debate over the relationship between missionaries and colonialists needs to be nuanced. In some instances they cooperated closely, while in others they clashed bitterly.

[11] Paul Gifford, ed., *The Christian Churches and the Democratization of Africa*, Leiden, E. J. Brill, 1995.

[12] Ndabaningi Sithole, *African Nationalism*, Oxford, Oxford University Press, 1959.

[13] Michael F. C. Bourdillon, *Religion and Society: A Text for Africa*, Gweru, Mambo Press, 1990.

provide services relating to HIV and AIDS. Thanks to the efforts of missionaries and African evangelists, the church is found in remote and inaccessible parts of the continent. It is an all-pervasive institution. Its buildings can be found on mountaintops and deep in river valleys. Among AICs taking on the missionary task, gatherings take place in the open and in sacred groves.[14] In Zimbabwe, all night vigils (*pungwe*) held across denominational lines promote ecumenism and announce the church's abiding presence in the community.[15] The church has provided meaning to generations of converts in Africa. Christianity has become part of the African identity.[16] Christian names for children, hymns and choruses for happy and sad occasions and the high visibility of Christian symbols all confirm the church's impact on the lives of people.

In addition, the church has bequeathed a sacred text to African communities.

The Bible in Africa

One of the most significant aspects of the Christian heritage in Africa has been the centrality of the Bible. As with other world religions, scripture plays an important role in the lives of believers. The Bible is highly read in African homes, schools and churches and on a variety of occasions. As John Mbiti states, 'Africa is deeply immersed in the Bible'.[17]

Lamin Sanneh has shown how the translation of the Bible into the vernacular had tremendous consequences for

---

[14] Terence Ranger, 'Taking on the Missionary Task: African Spirituality and the Mission Churches of Manicaland in the 1930s', in David Maxwell, ed., with Ingrid Lawrie, *Christianity and the African Imagination: Essays in Honour of Adrian Hastings*, Leiden, E. J. Brill, 2002.

[15] Titus Presler, *Transfigured Night: Mission and Culture in Zimbabwe's Vigil Movement*, Pretoria, UNISA, 1999.

[16] Terence Ranger, 'Religion, Development and African Christian Identity', in Kirsten Holst-Peterson, ed., *Religion, Development and African Identity*, Uppsala, Scandinavian Institute of African Studies, 1985.

[17] John S. Mbiti, 'Do You Understand What You are Reading? The Bible in African Homes, Schools and Churches', *Missionalia* 33, 2005, p. 247.

African Christianity. [18] Having the word of God in African languages helped a great deal in presenting Christianity as truly an African religion. The Bible continues to inspire the African imagination. Some creative writers, like Ngugi wa Thiong'o of Kenya, have utilized the biblical text in their work. [19]

As with other sacred writings, the Bible acts as a guide to belief and action. Children attending Sunday School proudly memorize and recite Bible verses. When theological differences arise between members of different denominations, appeals are made to the Bible for support. Preachers begin their sermons with Bible readings and cite biblical stories in their narratives. The Bible is used to comfort mourners, encourage students taking examinations and congratulate graduates. [20]

The church in Africa uses the Bible as a resource to meet all the exigencies of life. For communities that used to rely exclusively on orality, possessing a written sacred text has led both to excitement and apprehension. The excitement lies in the democratization of God's revelation: whereas previously only a few selected individuals had direct access to divine oracles, the new dispensation allows everyone access to the word of God. This has also created concerns about authority and interpretation. Who has the final say when the community holds different views over the most appropriate interpretation of a sacred text?

The church in Africa holds the Bible in high esteem and this valorization cuts across denominational lines. (However, as we shall see, some African women theologians have shown how the church has tended to support oppres-

---

[18] Lamin Sanneh, *Translating the Message: The Missionary Impact upon Culture*, Maryknoll, NY, Orbis Books, 1989.

[19] See Jesse N. K. Mugambi, *Critiques of Christianity in African Literature with Particular Reference to the East African Context*, Nairobi, East African Educational Publishers, 1992.

[20] For a detailed analysis of the Bible in Africa, see Gerald O. West and Musa W. Dube, eds, *The Bible in Africa: Transactions, Trajectories, Trends*, Boston, Brill, 2001.

sive patriarchal practices by citing the Bible.[21] They suggest there are 'other ways of reading the Bible'.)[22] The close parallels that exist between traditional African beliefs and practices and those described in the Old Testament enhance the attractiveness of the Bible for many African communities. Some, such as the Lemba/Remba of South Africa and Zimbabwe, the Abayudaya of Uganda and the Ibo in Nigeria, have claimed to be of ancient Israelite origin.[23]

The key role played by the Bible in Africa has major implications for the church's response to HIV and AIDS. As I shall show below, during the early stage of the epidemic, the Bible was often read in ways that did not affirm life. Many Christians turned to passages like 'For the wages of sin is death' (Romans 6:23) to account for the suffering and death of people with AIDS. Other readers utilized the Deuteronomistic view of history in which Yahweh rewards good and punishes evil. This initial reading of the Bible generated stigma and discrimination toward people living with HIV and AIDS. We are challenged to look again at Bible passages in life-affirming ways. This will enable the church to build on its strategic location in Africa.

A Legacy of Compassion

This section outlines some of the factors that provide the church with a firm basis for making an effective response to the HIV epidemic. They result from the history of African Christianity and place the church in a strategic position to provide leadership in the area of HIV and AIDS.

The Bible and the legacy of missionaries have combined to give the church in Africa a caring and compassionate face. Since its introduction, the church has been known to provide a safe place for marginalized members of the community. It was the mission station that offered refuge to young

---

[21] For example, Mercy Amba Oduyoye, *Daughters of Anowa: African Women and Patriarchy*, Maryknoll, NY, Orbis Books, 1995.

[22] Musa W. Dube, ed., *Other Ways of Reading: African Women and the Bible*, Geneva, World Council of Churches, 2001.

[23] Magdel le Roux, *The Lemba: A Lost Tribe of Israel in Southern Africa?* Pretoria, UNISA, 2003, p. 19.

girls running away from forced marriages. Missionaries welcomed individuals rejected by society due to traditional beliefs and practices. In Zimbabwe, for example, twins who would have been killed found refuge at mission stations.[24] The mission station came to be associated with refuge for all those to whom the African maxim 'I am because we are' did not bring relief. The church helped such individuals to have a new start in life.

The church in Africa has been associated with diakonia. It has provided free services to the most vulnerable social groups. Mission schools and hospitals have been open to the poorest of the poor. Promising students from less privileged backgrounds have had their studies financed by the church. It is the church that runs affordable schools in most parts of Africa. Mission education has been an integral part of the education system in Africa,[25] although some critics claim mission education has resulted in de-Africanization and that mission schools churn out people who hate their African identity.

The missionaries who cared for social outcasts illustrate the church's legacy of compassion in Africa. Individuals who suffered from leprosy were traditionally barred from interacting with other members of society because the disease was so highly contagious. In many African communities, such individuals were banished from their families and villages. They had special temporary shelters built for them outside the boundaries of the community. Food was brought to them in utensils that no one else used. They were truly cut off from everyone. Missionaries accepted them at mission stations. Mission hospitals provided care to individuals who had been forsaken by society.

Although African culture places emphasis on community, it is often ruthless towards individuals suspected of undermining social stability. One area where African culture is

---

[24] See the creative work of W. N. Mutasa, *Mapatya* (Twins), Salisbury, Longman Rhodesia, 1987.

[25] Gerrie Ter Haar, *Faith of Our Fathers: Studies on Religious Education in Sub-Saharan Africa*, Utrecht, Faculteit der Godgeleerdheid, 1990, p. 39.

particularly sensitive is witchcraft. As some studies have shown,[26] women are often at the receiving end of witchcraft accusations. Although there exist rituals of cleansing and reintegration, many women have endured violence and exclusion as a result. The church in Africa has taken care of such women. Mission stations have accepted women expelled from their communities on the basis of witchcraft accusations.

Following the example of Jesus who expressed solidarity with individuals and communities that were ostracized, the church in Africa has been associated with compassion. The church has looked after orphans and other vulnerable groups in different parts of Africa. It has been associated with charitable activities and humanitarian efforts. The era of HIV and AIDS presents new challenges for the church to reinforce its identity as a compassionate institution in Africa.

A Large Pool of Volunteers

One distinctive feature of religion is its capacity to recruit volunteers. At a time when the world places emphasis on financial security and rapid accumulation of wealth, religion continues to attract people who offer their voluntary services. The church in Africa has been very successful at mobilizing a large pool of volunteers. Although the gospel of prosperity encourages Christians to pursue material rewards, it also encourages the faithful to render free service to God.[27] Young African Pentecostals are actively involved in voluntary work, especially in urban areas. At many tertiary institutions, it is members of the different denominations who devote their time to fellow students with disabilities. They regard this is an integral part of their faith. In both rural and urban areas, Christians are well known for their willingness to give their time and effort without expecting any payment.

---

[26] Leny Lagerwerf, *Witchcraft, Sorcery and Spirit Possession: Pastoral in Africa*, Gweru, Mambo Press, 1987.

[27] Paul Gifford, *Ghana's New Christianity: Pentecostalism in a Globalizing African Economy*, London, Hurst, 2004.

The teaching of the church on giving without expecting anything in return has proved to be more effective than organizations that attempt to attract people by promising material rewards. Church women's organizations are especially significant in the provision of voluntary work. In Southern Africa they are known as *Manyano*. They are found in different denominations, each with its own uniform. These organizations provide women with a sense of belonging. In turn, the women live out their faith in dramatic fashion. While men have claimed to be too busy, it is the women from church who have answered the call to serve the poorest of the poor. They cook for and bathe the sick in their villages. They lead at funerals by consoling the bereaved and feeding the mourners (men only appear when they want to prove their authority, especially in designing the funeral programmes).

The voluntary work that women and men of faith in Africa undertake is never taken into account when national statistics are compiled. It goes unnoticed, principally because of the theology that informs Christian voluntary work. The service is not motivated by the need to be glorified by others but is seen as an act of worship. While some small NGOs in Africa magnify their accomplishments, the church is modest about its own considerable achievements.

The large pool of volunteers that the church in Africa can mobilize is a vital resource in the era of HIV and AIDS. As the Bible puts it, 'the harvest is plentiful, but the labourers are few' (Luke 10:2). At a time when the epidemic shows no signs of slowing down in most parts of Sub-Saharan Africa, the need for volunteers in the provision of care has never been greater. Grandmothers have had to be mothers all over again, due to the staggering number of orphans. Often, they perform this task with little or no resources.[28] Church volunteers in Africa can help stem the tide of HIV and AIDS.

---

[28] Neddy Matshalaga, *Grandmothers and Orphan Care in Zimbabwe*, Harare, SAFAIDS, 2004.

Highly Motivated Workers

The church in Africa can also boast highly motivated workers in many different roles and with various skills. Church-based NGOs also employ such workers. [29] These are people who are fired by their faith and commitment to Christian values. They bring this commitment to their work.

Of particular significance are medical personnel at mission hospitals. Medical missions have always been an integral part of the church in Africa. Missionaries regarded their task as one of bringing both the transforming power of the gospel (Romans 1:16) and the physical healing effected by Western medicine. Although critics rightly note that the missionaries' approach to health contradicted the holistic approach of Jesus and African culture, only the most radical of them would downplay the contribution of the church to the health delivery systems on the continent. Africans are now largely in charge at mission hospitals and they are carrying out their work with diligence and enthusiasm.

The highly motivated workers at church-related medical institutions are responsible for the popularity of these institutions. In most African countries, they are more popular than public health institutions. Health workers in church institutions are known to go beyond the call of duty. They are known to be caring and compassionate.

The church's highly motivated workforce is strategically placed to enable the church to be at the frontline in responding to HIV and AIDS. Whether it is schoolteachers in church-owned schools or medical personnel at hospitals, they can be expected to assist the church in its quest to become AIDS competent. Equally, workers in NGOs who are motivated by the Christian faith will be called upon to ensure that their messages relating to HIV and AIDS are communicated effectively. This will ensure that more

---

[29] Erica Bornstein, *The Spirit of Development: Protestant NGOs, Morality and Economics in Zimbabwe*, Palo Alto, CA, Stanford University Press, 2005.

people will receive the most accurate and up-to-date information about the epidemic.

An Abiding Presence in the Community

The church has been in Africa for a very long time – so long, in fact, that Christianity should now be considered an African religion.[30] However, it was only in the eighteenth and nineteenth centuries that most African countries started to have more established Christian communities.[31] Once the church became established in Africa, it did not take long for it to consolidate its presence. The combination of missionaries from Europe and North America and African evangelists ensured that the church became an integral part of the community. Although Christianity was introduced with all its Western baggage, it soon adopted an African worldview. African Christians now express their faith within their own cultural contexts.[32]

The church has become a crucial institution in many African countries. It is acknowledged as a significant social actor. Two key factors have worked in the church's favour: longevity and reliability. As postcolonial African states struggled to provide social services to their citizens, NGOs moved in. The corruption that characterized a number of postcolonial African states led to the emergence of such NGOs. These NGOs operate in various areas, sometimes complimenting the state, sometimes in opposition to it. Most of them have their head offices outside Africa. They regard Africa as a 'mission field'.

NGOs have made useful contributions to Africa's development. They have increased citizens' awareness of their rights on a continent where many states trample on them

---

[30] John S. Mbiti, *Introduction to African Religion*, London, Heinemann, 1975.

[31] Christianity in parts of Egypt and Ethiopia does not conform to this typology, as it was introduced much earlier and has had an unbroken presence.

[32] Harvey J. Sindima, *Drums of Redemption: An Introduction to African Christianity*, Westport, CT, Greenwood Press, 1994.

with impunity.[33] They have also been actively involved in issues related to children, women and the environment. Many are passionate about Africa's quest for development. However, unlike the church, the roots of most NGOs are not deep in the African soil.

In the face of HIV and AIDS, the church's endurance and credibility are a critical resource. Communities are more favourably disposed towards HIV and AIDS programmes run by the church because it has demonstrated its commitment. Communities have come to know and trust the church as an abiding presence, unlike some NGOs that run programmes for a fixed number of years. This is a major advantage that the church enjoys over other social actors in the context of HIV and AIDS. The epidemic requires long-term and sustainable responses. According to Peter Piot, who has served as a UNAIDS executive:

> Political systems come and go, politicians, businesses and UN organizations come and go, but the long-term perspective, the memory and the future is with faith-based organizations and religions ... that perspective is what has been missing in our response to the AIDS epidemic.[34]

Credibility

Admittedly, the church in Africa is not immune to scandal, including rape and violence against women and children, church leaders who refuse to leave office at the end of their contracts, abuse of funds and other 'worldly' misdeeds. In some of its theological pronouncements, the church has also sometimes found itself supporting oppression. The

---

[33] Mahmood Mamdani, *Citizen and Subject: Contemporary Africa and the Legacy of Late Colonialism*, Princeton, NJ, Princeton University Press, 1996.

[34] Peter Piot, in N. Ndugane, 'The Challenge of HIV/AIDS to Christian Theology', conference paper, University of Western Cape, 30 July 2004, p. 9; cited in Jill Olivier, 'Where Does the Christian Stand? Considering a Public Discourse of Hope in the Context of HIV/AIDS in South Africa', *Journal of Theology for Southern Africa* 126, 2006, p. 95.

church in South Africa, Zimbabwe and Namibia was compromised when it sided with white minority regimes.[35]

Despite such evils and weaknesses, the church has been identified as a consistent supporter of marginalized individuals and communities. In those countries where the church was part and parcel of institutional racism, many individuals defied their superiors and contributed to the struggle for liberation. Communities in Africa have tended to make a distinction between the failings of individuals and the church as a theological construct. Consequently, they have retained faith in the church even when its functionaries have shown serious character flaws.

The church is regarded as a highly reliable social institution in Africa. Its pronouncements on various ethical issues are taken seriously. It is not only church members who pay attention when it announces its position on a particular issue. Other members of the community who do not necessarily subscribe to the Christian faith also recognize the church's moral authority. They regard it as having the credibility to take a stance on various issues.

The dependability of the church in Africa puts it in a strategic position to tackle HIV and AIDS. The leadership of the church can make use of the pulpit to disseminate information relating to HIV and AIDS prevention and care. They can also increase the knowledge of treatment among their members by providing the latest information regarding antiretroviral drugs. Their messages will be well received, as the audience already considers them as representatives of a credible institution.

The church's credibility in Africa is due to its many pro-poor programmes. When it proclaims messages that affect the lives of people, the community takes notice. The church should therefore capitalize on its credibility to promote life in the context of HIV and AIDS. When the church takes a life-affirming stance on HIV and AIDS prevention, treatment and care communities can be galvanized into action.

[35] See, for example, John W. De Gruchy, *The Church Struggle in South Africa*, Cape Town, David Phillip, 1979.

They, too, recognize the church as a dynamic and credible institution that should stand for life. Ronald Nicolson is right: 'churches are still widely trusted as reliable sources of education.'[36]

Membership from Diverse Professional Backgrounds

An ecclesiology that dwells on ordained members prevents most people from realizing that the church is home to people from various walks of life. This is a remarkable fact that needs to be fully appreciated. The church in Africa enjoys the membership of people with different areas of specialization. These include artisans, medical personnel, politicians, economists and theologians. It is unfortunate that the church rarely calls upon their expertise in a direct way. In most instances, their membership is appreciated only to the extent that they make financial contributions that help to support the church's activities.

The era of HIV challenges the church in Africa to take an inventory of the human resources at its disposal. The church needs to devise creative channels to ensure that its members make optimum use of its infrastructure. With their diverse skills, members can achieve impressive results in their responses to the epidemic. For example, church members skilled in medicine and teaching could be asked to use church premises to impart basic knowledge about HIV and AIDS prevention, treatment and care. Experience has shown that many people with such expertise are willing to volunteer, as they feel they are contributing meaningfully to the life of the church.

The church in Africa continues to struggle to be self-sufficient. In the 1960s and 1970s, the moratorium debate saw the African church making strong pronouncements against foreign funding.[37] The HIV epidemic has since placed a great burden on the church's resources. Programmes can be expensive to run. Caring for the sick and the affected is

[36] Ronald Nicolson, *AIDS: A Christian Response*, Pietermaritzburg, Cluster Publications, 1995, p. 6.

[37] See, for example, Samuel Kobia, *The Courage to Hope: A Challenge for Churches in Africa*, Nairobi, Acton Publishers, 2003, pp. 131–2.

a costly exercise. The church needs to utilize the expertise of its members to devise cost-effective strategies to mitigate the effects of HIV and AIDS. It needs to draw on its economic planners, accountants and other specialists to enable it to run sustainable projects.

Too often, the church has looked outside itself for specialists. It has also tended to regard its own message and mission as targeting those who are outside. *Outreach* has been the key term. The HIV epidemic calls for a paradigm shift. There is an urgent need for *inreach*. The church needs to preach to the converted in this time of HIV and AIDS.[38] It also needs to tap its own human resources.

Prayer and Spirituality

The church in Africa has a vibrant prayerful and spiritual life. This is also a valuable resource in the response to HIV and AIDS. NGOs and government agencies are often constrained when it comes to acknowledging the importance of prayer in the response to the HIV epidemic. The church is privileged to have prayer and spirituality as key resources in its life. Many people in hospitals and homes across Africa have been relieved to receive Christians who say prayers for them. They have regained their strength and capacity to face their situations with courage and hope.[39]

For many African Christians, prayer is the church's unique contribution to the overall response to HIV and AIDS. As this book will emphasize, the 'ministry of presence' is critical to the church's contribution to the struggle against the epidemic. Across Africa, Christians have been united in praying for breakthroughs in scientific researches on prevention and treatment. Churches have preached messages of love, healing and hope. Many Christians have given generously to causes that seek to assist orphans and other vulnerable children. They recognize the importance of prayer, faith and hope in the church's response to the

---

[38] Musa W. Dube, 'Preaching to the Converted: Unsettling the Christian Church', *Ministerial Formation* 93, 2001, pp. 38–50.

[39] This evokes the title of Samuel Kobia's book, *The Courage to Hope*.

epidemic. It is therefore crucial for the church to continue to place emphasis on prayer and spirituality in the era of HIV and AIDS. [40]

Prayer and spirituality need to be emphasized because they set the churches apart from secular NGOs. Churches in Africa must utilize this resource with a lot of responsibility. As they visit the sick and console the bereaved, African churches must continue to provide hope.

Conclusion

The church in Africa possesses immense potential to respond effectively to HIV and AIDS. In many places it has been actively involved in the struggle against the epidemic. Such efforts need to be scaled up and supported to ensure their sustainability in the long run.

> The world's religions reach out to virtually every community in the most remote corners of the earth. According to the director of the Medical Assistance Programme (MAP) International, religion plays a central, integrating role in social and cultural life in most developing countries. In many countries, there are more religious leaders and workers in faith-based organizations (FBOs) than health workers. They are in close and regular contact with all age groups in society and their voice is highly respected. In traditional communities, religious leaders are often more influential than local government officials, secular community leaders and health professionals. [41]

---

[40] See, for example, Sara Woldehanna et al., *Faith in Action: Examining the Role of Faith-Based Organizations in Addressing HIV/AIDS: A Multi-Country, Key Informant Survey*, Washington, DC, Global Health Council, 2005, p. 33.

[41] Georges Tiendrebeogo and Michael Buykx, *Faith-Based Organizations and HIV/AIDS Prevention and Impact Mitigation in Africa*, Amsterdam, Royal Tropical Institute, 2004, p. 17.

Chapter 2
A Weakened Response to HIV/AIDS

Chapter one highlighted numerous factors that equip the church in Africa to provide an effective response to HIV and AIDS. In addition, however, in the quest to become AIDS competent, the church needs to adopt an honest and self-critical stance. It needs to recognize that despite its remarkable strengths, there are many factors that have weakened its response to the epidemic.

This chapter outlines some of these major weaknesses. If the church faces them with openness, it can provide a more effective response. What the church in Africa cannot afford to do in the context of HIV is to refuse to accept criticism. It is only through constant self-evaluation that improvements can be made. The criticisms noted in this chapter are meant to challenge the church to aspire to excellence.

Stigma and Discrimination

When the HIV epidemic first broke out in Africa in the 1980s, the church fuelled stigma and discrimination. The Bible was read in ways that condemned people living with HIV. The issue was simplistically reduced to one of individual or personal morality. Vulnerability to infection was understood solely in terms of whether or not one was sexually promiscuous. People living with HIV were regarded as individuals who did not live up to the high moral standards set by the church.

Such stigma continues to be a major problem, especially as the most common route of HIV transmission in Sub-Saharan Africa has been through sex between men and women. As Gillian Paterson observes, 'HIV and AIDS are linked in people's minds with sex, sexuality and sexual orientation: all of which are associated in Christian tradition with sin.'[42] This has worsened the stigma that people living with HIV face. In her review of the responses of FBOs to HIV and AIDS in Sub-Saharan Africa, Sue Parry notes that

---

[42] Gillian Paterson, *AIDS-Related Stigma: Thinking Outside the Box: The Theological Challenge*, Geneva, Ecumenical Advocacy Alliance, 2005, p. 9.

20

'a culture of silence, denial, stigma and discrimination has largely been the response'. [43]

Donald Messer cites Jonathan Mann, the first director of the World Health Organization Global Programme on AIDS, who suggests that every person or society undergoes three stages of reaction to HIV and AIDS:

1 Denial of the problem.

2 Minimization of the problem's significance.

3 Emergence of constructive engagement to resolve the challenges. [44]

It is indeed unfortunate that the church has taken far too long to reach the stage of constructive engagement to resolve the challenge posed by HIV and AIDS.

The tendency to reduce HIV and AIDS to the issue of personal morality has in many ways prevented the church from being the welcoming and loving community it is meant to be. The initial response was to suggest an artificial separation between *us* and *them*. The church characterized HIV as belonging to the 'sinners in the world'. According to this stance, the church, a pure and holy institution, was not affected. This led to the branding of people living with HIV:

> Being branded is like being put in a 'box' that is often or always associated with something negative or undesirable. Branding limits a person's ability to be seen as a worthy human being with different qualities and characteristics. Somebody who has been branded is looked upon as different in an undesirable manner. Branding puts people on the outside of groups and communities. A more formal word for branding is stigmatization. [45]

The church has made some appreciable gains in denouncing HIV and AIDS stigma. Some denominations have devel-

[43] Sue Parry, *Responses of the Faith-Based Organizations to HIV/AIDS in Southern Africa*, Geneva, World Council of Churches, 2003, p. 11.

[44] Donald E. Messer, *Breaking the Conspiracy of Silence: Christian Churches and the Global AIDS Crisis*, Minneapolis, Fortress Press, 2004, pp. 5–6.

[45] Elisabeth Tveito and Estrid Hessellund, eds, *Positive-Branding Sexuality, HIV and AIDS*, Oslo, Church of Norway Council on Ecumenical and International Relations/Development Education Service, 2005, p. 15.

oped and implemented HIV and AIDS policies. Some have denounced it as a sin to stigmatize people living with HIV. Many church members support orphans and other vulnerable children. In some congregations, people living with HIV are openly embraced. However, stigma continues to hinder the church's efforts to counter HIV and AIDS. This has been worsened by theological rigidity.

Theological Rigidity

The church's mission is to proclaim the good news of Jesus Christ to the entire human race. It holds certain truths as immutable. Critical to its understanding of salvation history is that the Word became flesh (John 1:14). It strives to be consistent in its proclamation. It understands its mission as preserving the self-revelation of God throughout the ages, to the end of time. This is why the creedal formula 'As it was in the beginning, is now and ever shall be' gives the church the assurance of consistency.

While the church definitely needs to hold on to basic truths, the era of HIV calls for a fresh understanding of these truths. It was perhaps inevitable for the church to frame its initial response to the epidemic in existing theological vocabulary. HIV became a manifestation of humanity's sinfulness. The epidemic was interpreted as fulfilling the curses cited in Deuteronomy 28:27, which include God sending incurable diseases to an apostate people. HIV was read as a signifier that the end of the world was drawing near (Luke 21:5–28). The failure to develop a vaccine to cure HIV has been taken by some as confirming God's punishment of a stubborn and sinful generation.

In traditional theology, God rewards good and punishes evil. HIV is attributed to humanity's refusal to follow God's commandments. Promiscuity and rebelliousness in all its forms are the reasons why the epidemic exists, according to this line of thinking. Theological rigidity and intellectual aridity have led to the church's failure to interpret HIV and AIDS as a critical turning point.

HIV and AIDS is arguably the sign of the times in Sub-Saharan Africa, and particularly in Southern Africa, at the beginning of the new millennium. It is a sign of crisis, and also of opportunity, a sign of desperation, and also of hope. It is very easy to get caught up in the negativity and hopelessness of the HIV and AIDS pandemic as it manifests itself around us and yet the challenge to us as church and society is profound. We, the people of God, the suffering body of Christ, are being called and invited, challenged and urged, to live our common humanity, to be wounded proclaimers of the kingdom of God among a people that is struggling with its identity, its beliefs, its values.[46]

The church, from its leadership to its laity, has taken a long time to realize that the HIV epidemic represents a crucial theological turning point. It is no longer possible to derive satisfaction from the old answers. Neither will it do to apply simplistically the tired old category of 'sinners' in the context of the devastation caused by HIV and AIDS. When wailing and lamentation become daily experiences in some African villages and cities, hard theological questions that require fresh answers are prompted. Some of the questions are abiding ones, and they require creative responses.

Here are some of the questions that emerge from the cemeteries that are rapidly filling with the bodies of young people in Africa:

- Where is God when so many people are dying?

- Where is the love of Jesus Christ when some mothers have lost eight dear children to AIDS?

- How comforting is the presence of the Holy Spirit to orphaned children who face uncertain futures?

Instead of retreating into the shell of theological rigidity, the church in Africa needs to ask these hard questions. Nobody should be left off the hook.[47]

[46] Alison Munro, 'Responsibility: The Prevention of HIV/AIDS', in Stuart C. Bate, ed., *Responsibility in a Time of AIDS: A Pastoral Response by Catholic Theologians and AIDS Activists in Southern Africa*, Linden, St Augustine's College of South Africa, 2003, p. 32.

[47] Edward P. Antonio, a Zimbabwean theologian, used this phrase at a session during the American Academy of Religion Annual Meeting in Philadelphia, 19–24 November 2005.

Theological rigidity accounts for the slow pace of the church in Africa in its move to the frontlines of the struggle against HIV. While the church wasted valuable time debating the morality of condoms, for example, precious lives were lost. While it embraced HIV as God's punishment to an apostate generation, it drove some among us with AIDS prematurely to their graves. While it composed more funeral choruses, it choked the life out of some people who could have held on. When some fiery preachers mocked people with AIDS, they thereby alienated them from the commonwealth of the new Israel (Ephesians 4:18).

It is theological rigidity that has prevented the church in Africa from taking structural sin seriously in HIV and AIDS discourses. Traditional theology tends to place emphasis on individual sin. It dwells on moral failure by individuals. In contexts of HIV, it readily blames the individual who becomes infected for failing to uphold the high moral standards set by the church. However, we need to pay attention to unjust *systems* that increase vulnerability to HIV and AIDS. The World Council of Church's study document *Facing AIDS* provides a detailed overview of these factors:

> At the root of the global socioeconomic and cultural problems related to HIV and AIDS are the unjust distribution and accumulation of wealth, land and power. This leads to various forms of malaise in human communities. There are more cases of economic and political migration of people within and outside of their own countries. These uprooted peoples may be migrant workers looking for better-paying jobs or refugees from economic, political or religious conflicts. Racism, gender discrimination and sexual harassment, economic inequalities, the lack of political will for change, huge external and internal debts, critical health problems, illicit drugs and sex trades, including an increase in child prostitution, fragmentation and marginalization of communities – all these factors, which affect 'developed' as well as 'developing' societies, form a web of interrelated global problems which intensify the vulnerability of human communities to HIV and AIDS. [48]

[48] World Council of Churches, *Facing AIDS: The Challenge: The Churches' Response*, Geneva, World Council of Churches, 1997, pp. 14–15.

Theological rigidity is overcome when the church demonstrates its willingness to address these 'drivers and co-determinants' of the epidemic. It must be courageous to tackle poverty, gender inequity and the skewed global economic system. The church in Africa must be willing to accept that vulnerability to HIV infection goes far beyond individual morality. Thus:

> Vulnerable for HIV infection are people who, due to limited self-determination in social, sexual and other areas, have an increased risk of HIV infection: women, children, CSWs [commercial sex workers], homosexuals, young people, drug users, migrants, ethnic minorities and poor people. [49]

Theological rigidity has often immobilized the church and prevented it from conducting its mission in contexts of HIV and AIDS in the manner of Jesus. Just as Jesus interacted with the marginalized groups of his day – women, children, lepers, tax collectors, sex workers, the Samaritans and others – so too does the church of today need to engage in mission at the edges of society. The church in Africa needs to interact with men who have sex with men, sex workers, and other marginalized groups. It needs to increase levels of HIV and AIDS awareness among such groups, while demonstrating its love and acceptance.

One strategy to help the church break through this theological rigidity is to train and retrain its ministers in the area of HIV. Some older pastors do not possess adequate information on the epidemic. At a preachers' workshop in Tsholotsho, rural Zimbabwe in 2006, one pastor described HIV and AIDS as 'that disease one gets from South Africa'. He was convinced that AIDS was not a Zimbabwean reality. Other misconceptions about the epidemic are common among pastors.

It has been difficult for the church in Africa to make significant theological breakthroughs on HIV because its theologians have struggled to come to terms with the epi-

[49] Sonja Weinreich and Christoph Benn, *AIDS: Meeting the Challenge*, Geneva, World Council of Churches, 2004, p. 21.

demic. Leading African male theologians like John S. Mbiti, Kwame Bediako and others have not addressed HIV and AIDS in their works. Tinyiko Sam Maluleke, a South African black theologian, argues that HIV caught the African theological fraternity off-guard:

> In fact, just as we were becoming comfortable in our new-found voice for black and African theologies; just as African evangelicals and Pentecostalism were declaring this to be a century in which all Africans will be 'reached' for Christ; just as some Africans were celebrating the end of the cold war and the end of apartheid – the AIDS pandemic comes along and makes a mockery of many of our hopes and claims, sending us all into a deep crisis. [50]

The deep crisis that Maluleke identifies has been keenly felt in the preaching of the church on HIV and AIDS. Although some individual ministers have been creative in their pastoral response to the epidemic, many have turned churches into 'no-go' areas for those of us living with HIV. The sermons preached by some pastors pierce into the inner recesses of the hearts of those of us living with HIV. Their message is suffocating and paralysing. Whereas those of us living with HIV expect the church to accompany them, we are sent off on a lonely journey without a return ticket! Whereas those of us living with HIV look forward to a safe place of respite, we meet hostility and ostracism. People who are living positively and look for acceptance and understanding, instead encounter rejection and condemnation.

As the church in Africa strives to become AIDS competent, it needs to develop a life-affirming theology of HIV. It must become a haven of belonging to those of us living with HIV. The church in Africa needs to come out of the Egypt of theological rigidity into the Canaan of theological creativity as it seeks to respond to HIV. It needs to recognize that the

---

[50] Tinyiko Sam Maluleke, 'Towards an HIV/AIDS-Sensitive Curriculum', in Musa W. Dube, ed., *HIV/AIDS and the Curriculum: Methods of Integrating HIV/AIDS in Theological Programmes*, Geneva, World Council of Churches, 2003, p. 61.

epidemic provides a significant moment for undertaking deep theological reflection. Building on Maluleke's insight cited above, the South African scholar Beverley Haddad observes:

> For our current context provides us with both a moment of truth in critical and dangerous times as well as a moment of grace and opportunity. Yes, we live in critical and dangerous times and our HIV positive world challenges our theology, our traditions, and our cultures. It forces us to seek new understandings of God and of God's work in the world and to find ways of living as 'church' that are redemptive to both men and women. [51]

Overcoming theological rigidity will enable the church to unlock its vast potential and equip it to stem the tide of HIV in Africa. This limitation needs to be overcome, as it has prevented the church from mounting effective and durable programmes. The church has not been able to provide the necessary leadership in the struggle against HIV because it has not been able to shake off its theological rigidity.

Insensitivity to Gender Issues

Alongside theological rigidity, the church in Africa's response to the HIV epidemic has been blunted by its general insensitivity towards the issue of gender. As many studies have shown, gender inequality is one of the major factors driving the epidemic in most parts of Sub-Saharan Africa. Women's vulnerability to HIV infection has been identified as a key issue. However, the church in Africa remains the bastion of patriarchy and male privilege. African women 'groan in faith'. [52]

The church has struggled to take up the issue of gender justice in contexts of HIV because the church itself has not fully embraced the cause. The Bible continues to be read in

---

[51] Beverley Haddad, 'We Pray But We Cannot Heal: Theological Challenges Posed by the HIV/AIDS Crisis', *Journal of Theology for Southern Africa*, 125, 2006, p. 81.

[52] Musimbi R. Kanyoro and Nyambura J. Njoroge, eds, *Groaning in Faith: African Women in the Household of God*, Nairobi, Acton, 1996.

ways that promote patriarchy. Women in abusive relationships continue to be sacrificed for the sake of upholding
the sacrality of marriage. Single women who head families
struggle to gain acceptance in church. For some, the Mothers Unions or Manyano in South Africa provide space for
churchwomen to express themselves. Thus:

> Without space on the pulpit and in the lecture halls, many
> women use the prayer time and prayer space for the *Man-
> yano* meetings to express themselves and their dreams for the
> church. It is in these groups that other women in the faith nur-
> ture young women. Clad in their uniforms, these women feel
> different and inspired to speak, sing and act in courageous ways
> that they would not otherwise have done. In these times of the
> HIV and AIDS pandemic, the pastoral and prayer-like focus of
> the *Manyano* has become even more important. In these *Man-
> yano* meetings people meet to sing, pray and cry together in
> local denominational circles of dignity and defiance. [53]

In the above quotation, Brigalia Bam shows that such
groups provide women with alternative spaces where they
have greater latitude to express themselves. Squeezed by
patriarchal dictates in the formal structures of the church,
African churchwomen turn to their own organizations to
find a place to feel at home. Bam celebrates women's groups
as a positive step towards the liberation of African Christian women.

I am an African male scholar of religion and am thus
heavily implicated in the subordination of women. Patriarchy grants me many privileges that I often take for granted.
Consequently, I need to engage in considerable reflexivity
before critiquing women's groups and their contribution
to the struggle against HIV. This critique is informed by
the conviction that women's groups provide the most valuable component of the church in Africa. How the Mothers
Unions react to HIV goes a long way in determining the
overall response of the church.

---

[53] Brigalia Bam, 'Women and the Church in (South) Africa: Women are
the Church in (South) Africa', in Isabel Apawo Phiri and Sarojini Nadar,
eds, *On Being Church: African Women's Voices and Visions*, Geneva, World
Council of Churches, 2005, p. 13.

It needs to be acknowledged that churchwomen's groups are the most visible expression of African Christianity. In their various uniforms, they provide colour and vibrancy to the church on the continent. Their charitable activities in both rural and urban areas are noteworthy.[54] It is the members of the Mothers Unions who are visible on the frontlines – at weddings, funerals, conferences and so on. However, as Bam shows, power remains firmly in the hands of men. The major question is: how can churchwomen's organizations in Africa be transformed to make them more effective in the face of HIV?

First, there is an urgent need to ensure that churchwomen's groups in Africa become acutely aware of HIV issues. These include the vulnerability of married women and the prevention options that are available, including the female condom. Organizations like the Circle of Concerned African Women Theologians (the Circle) play a leading role in this regard. Too many married, decent and God-fearing women have been sacrificed in the name of 'respecting' their husbands. Women's groups within the church in Africa need to be empowered to resist and critique patriarchy.

Second, women's groups in church need to be equipped to read the Bible in a liberating way. As we have already seen, the reality of HIV necessitates a rereading of the Bible. Can one still read the passage on the virtuous woman in Proverbs 31:10–31 innocently in the era of HIV?[55] Should women's groups continue to be exclusively exposed to male heroes in the biblical text? Should churchwomen's groups encourage women to suffer in silence when their husbands expose them to HIV infection? Women of faith in Africa need to read the Bible in ways that are life affirming. This implies placing emphasis on those stories that show women's resis-

---

[54] See, for example, Ezra Chitando, '"There was at Joppa a Disciple": A Study of the Participation of Women in a Rural Assembly in Zimbabwe', *Journal of Constructive Theology* 4, 1, 1998, pp. 73–88.

[55] Ezra Chitando, 'The Good Wife: A Phenomenological Rereading of Proverbs 31:10–31 in the Context of HIV/AIDS in Zimbabwe', *Scriptura* 86, 2, 2004, pp. 151–9.

tance to death-dealing practices, while deconstructing those accounts that promote women's vulnerability to HIV.

Third, women's groups in church must be centres of constant and rigorous critiques of patriarchy. Too often, leaders of churchwomen's groups have uncritically endorsed patriarchal values and dictates. In some denominations, the politics of who puts on the uniform reflects patriarchal definitions of the 'good wife'. Furthermore, the continuing marginalization of single women is an indictment of the organizations' lack of commitment to gender justice. The celebration of being 'Mrs Somebody' forces many single women (some of them young widows due to HIV and AIDS) to experience the church as an exclusive club for married people.

Fourth, the strengthening of sisterly solidarity among churchwomen in Africa will lead to greater competence in the face of HIV. Solidarity implies standing shoulder to shoulder with all women, regardless of their denomination and marital or other status. It means identifying with sex workers, abused teenage girls and the young women who work as maids or helpers. Churchwomen's groups in Africa need to move beyond the paradigm of being 'respectable and responsible' women to one that entails a radical mission of empowering vulnerable women to face HIV.

It is clear that it is women's groups that will demonstrate the church in Africa's commitment to gender justice in the face of HIV. However, it is deeply unfair to place all the burden and responsibility upon the shoulders of women of faith. As the writings by the Circle show, women in Africa are already carrying heavy burdens. Without reducing them to hapless victims, we can acknowledge that they face formidable odds. Patriarchy threatens to paralyse them, while the global economic system chokes them. It is therefore important that other actors be actively involved in the implementation of projects that will sharpen the church's gender sensitivity.

30

Reclaiming the Meaning of Gender: Engaging Men in HIV and AIDS Issues

There is now an urgent need for the church in Africa to address aggressive masculinities. The continued neglect of men in HIV awareness and prevention campaigns has led to disappointing results for FBOs, NGOs and the public sector. If the church is to become more gender sensitive, it needs to mount credible and effective programmes that target men. When men are left out, programmes will achieve only partial success. The following passage summarizes the experience thus far:

> Development programmes have tried to focus on women and on improving their livelihood in order to make them more independent from men. This has succeeded only to a certain extent. Due to sociocultural factors, women are often not allowed to decide of their own volition how the money they earn should be used. Also, some organizations have noticed that by focusing on women and leaving men 'out of the picture', any gain in the economic status of women has often been met with jealousy on the part of men, which has sometimes expressed itself in an increase of domestic violence. One crucial factor will always be the relationship between women and men. Only if there is a change in this dynamic, leading to mutual respect and understanding, and only if women have the same rights as men and are able to act on these rights, will women be able to also protect themselves successfully against an HIV infection.[56]

By addressing men, the church in Africa will be filling a massive gap in HIV and AIDS intervention programmes. Most NGOs on the continent have focused on the vulnerability of women and children. This has left men outside the scope of most HIV and AIDS programmes. Only a few NGOs, like Padare/Men's Forum on Gender and Engender Health, have a clear mandate to address men's issues. While womanist theologians might feel that men, as their erstwhile oppressors and beneficiaries of patriarchy, do not

---

[56] Astrid Berner-Rodoreda, *HIV and AIDS in Africa – A Female Epidemic Requiring Only a Female Response? The Gender Dimension of HIV and AIDS in Africa and Good Practical Examples from Partner Organizations of Bread for the World*, Stuttgart, Bread for the World, 2006, p. 13.

deserve particular attention, such a stance is unhelpful in the long run. Men, too, need liberation from patriarchy. The context of HIV and AIDS calls for a deconstruction of aggressive masculinities that lead men to have multiple sexual partners, perpetrate violence against women and engage in risky pursuits. [57]

The challenge that the church in Africa faces with regard to gender has undermined its effectiveness in responding to HIV and AIDS. Due to its own patriarchal outlook, the church has not provided a space conducive to women's self-expression. As a result, women's groups have emerged where women put into place an alternative model of being church. The church in Africa needs to face the gender question with creativity and boldness if it is to become fully AIDS competent.

Negative Attitudes Towards Sexuality

The church in Africa struggles to address the subject of human sexuality in an open and liberating way. This is a result of three main factors.

First, the nature of the faith that the missionaries bequeathed to the African church is anti-sexuality. As products of their own time, the missionaries who carried the gospel to African shores had a negative attitude towards human sexuality. This strand is of cause traceable to the early church. [58] The emergence of Christianity in the Greco-Roman empire meant that it was caught up in the debate between the flesh and the spirit. For some, the flesh was weak and constituted a stumbling block to the attainment of salvation. The apostle Paul subscribed to this school of thought to a considerable extent. He was convinced that celibacy offered a better path to spirituality and believed

---

[57] The second book in this series, *Acting in Hope*, discusses this theme in considerable detail. For an exposition on masculinities in Southern Africa, see Robert Morrell, ed., *Changing Men in Southern Africa*, Pietermaritzburg, University of Natal Press, 2001.

[58] See, for example, Agrippa G. Kathide, 'Teaching and Talking About Our Sexuality: A Means of Combating HIV/AIDS', in Dube, *HIV/AIDS and the Curriculum*, p. 5.

32

that marriage was a necessary concession due to the weakness of the human body (1 Corinthians 7:1–2).

Sexuality has tended to be associated with primordial sin in Christianity and sexual offences ranked as the worst type of sin humans can commit. Christianity is not alone in this, of course. Ifi Amadiume, a leading African gender specialist, observes that all cultures and religions regulate sex, although they permit some sexual freedom.[59] In Christianity in Africa, the emphasis has been on sex for procreation. Sex as pleasure is therefore a problematic area for the church in Africa.

Second, the inherited gospel in African Christianity has problematic assumptions. Some missionaries regarded the control of passion as one of their major tasks. They considered blacks as a race characterized by rampant sexual immorality. The encounter between whites and blacks was also expressed in terms of 'restrained' sexuality and 'loose' sexuality.[60] In their preaching, missionaries castigated the Africans' (supposed) servitude to the pleasures of the flesh. Africa could only be saved if it adopted the higher sexual morality contained in the gospel. According to Heike Becker, 'For some, particularly the missions, African sexuality was, and had always been, "primitive", uncontrolled and excessive, and as such it represented the darkness and dangers of the continent.'[61] It is important to note that this negative attitude towards sexuality was not confined to Africa; the church has been hesitant to address sexuality realistically in other parts of the world, too.

Third, the combination of Christianity, colonialism and modernity has had a negative impact on the indigenous African culture in relation to sexuality. Whereas previ-

[59] Ifi Amadiume, 'Sexuality, African Religio-Cultural Traditions and Modernity: Expanding the Lens', *CODESRIA Bulletin* 1 & 2, 2006, p. 26.

[60] For a useful discussion, see Maria Eriksson Baaz and Mai Palmberg, eds, *Same and Other: Negotiating African Identity in Cultural Production*, Uppsala, Nordiska Africa Institute, 2001.

[61] Heike Becker, '*Efundula:* Women's Initiation, Gender and Sexual Identities in Colonial and Post-Colonial Northern Namibia', in Signe Arnfred, ed., *Re-Thinking Sexualities in Africa*, Uppsala, Nordiska Africa Institute, 2004, p. 37.

ously initiation schools provided a platform for imparting sex education to young adults, these schools are no longer active in most places. As a result, there is growing uneasiness about talking publicly about sexuality in traditional culture. Before the negative impact of Christianity, sexuality was tackled effectively, with consideration for age, marital status and other variables.[62] To say this is not to glorify a dead African past but to indicate the burden of history in responding to HIV. The church in Africa needs to develop creative ways of tackling the issue of sexuality in the face of HIV.

All these factors have left the church in Africa without the vocabulary to address the theme of sexuality. This is a major limitation given that heterosexual transmission lies behind the rapid spread of HIV in Africa. The church in Africa has struggled to address the issue of human sexuality in an open and liberating way. It needs to utilize cultural resources to open up debate on the theme in the quest to preserve life.

Nothing should be more sacrosanct than protecting human life. This principle should be the guiding one. Theological creativity demands that the church upholds whatever promotes life and actively opposes whatever diminishes life. If this means going against some aspect of African culture, then so be it. Fortunately, African culture itself offers so many opportunities for addressing sexuality in effective ways. One way is to utilize rites of passages to impart knowledge about HIV. It is also possible to engage traditional leaders like chiefs, traditional healers and others to provide information on HIV.

By overcoming an impoverished gospel that demonizes sexuality and the cultural conservatism surrounding it, the church in Africa can become more effective in meeting the challenge of HIV. Youth groups, women's and men's groups, couples' and other special groups need to hear informed and clear messages on sexuality. Powerful sermons that

---

[62] Eunice K. Kamaara, *Gender, Youth Sexuality and HIV/AIDS: A Kenyan Experience*, Eldoret, AMECEA Gaba Publications, 2005, p. 10.

characterize sexual excitement as the devil's key weapon will not be effective if they are not backed by practical suggestions on handling sexual desire to young and old people. The reference to old people is deliberate, as some people tend to forget that they, too, have sexual feelings.

Christians, including those who uphold celibacy, are not 'frozen virgins'. The sexual drive is one of the most powerful impulses of the human body. The church in Africa needs to acknowledge this reality and engage it in a sensitive way. It needs to interrogate its negative attitude towards human sexuality. It must embrace sexuality as a gift of God:

> In becoming a redemptive community, we need to begin to celebrate our sexuality as a gift from God. The traditions of the church have notoriously seen sexuality as 'dangerous', thus rendering it a taboo subject confined to the secret and dark corners of our lives. The silence becomes even more deafening given the lack of analysis of patriarchy and gender injustice within the church and society. Engaging in theological discussions concerning HIV prevention in an honest and culturally sensitive way becomes difficult. Ministry in an HIV positive world means that the church needs to be a place where sexuality is celebrated in its goodness and challenged where it brings death. [63]

External Dependency

External dependency is one significant drawback that the church in Africa faces in its quest to become AIDS competent. Many AICs and African Pentecostal churches have been able to overcome this limitation. [64] However, the 'mainline' churches continue to have mother–daughter relationships with churches in Europe and North America. They depend on external resources for their projects. Their HIV and AIDS projects are often financed from abroad.

One does not wish to downplay the practical and theological significance of sharing resources within the global

---

[63] Beverley Haddad, 'We Pray But We Cannot Heal', p. 89.

[64] In fact, many AICs and African Pentecostal churches support missions in Europe and North America using resources mobilized in Africa. (Personal communication by Afe Adogame, Bayreuth, Germany, 29 August 2005.)

church. This demonstrates solidarity between the North and the South within the church. However, the church in Africa needs to be more actively involved in mobilizing resources from within. Continuing to rely on external resources perpetuates the negative image of Africa as a poor and desperate continent. There are compelling theological, political and economic reasons for the church in Africa to become financially independent.

External dependency prevents the church in Africa from maximizing locally available resources in responding to HIV and AIDS. A dependency syndrome stifles the church's capacity to raise resources locally. While it remains critical for the church to access the 'big money', experience has shown that many successful HIV and AIDS projects are run on modest budgets. There is an urgent need for resource mobilization in the era of HIV and AIDS. The task is so demanding that it should not be left to the whims of parishioners in faraway countries.

As noted above, African Pentecostals and AICs have led the way in raising money at the parish/assembly level. Granted that some pastors have pushed their congregants too far with the chant of 'giving and giving', one should acknowledge their emphasis on financial autonomy. African Pentecostal churches have equipped their members with the right attitude regarding the need for self-sufficiency at the local level. If adequate financial control systems are put in place, these congregations are financially empowered to run viable HIV and AIDS programmes. They are equipped to look after the nutritional needs of people living with AIDS, as well as to support orphans and other vulnerable children.

Overcoming dependence on external sources will enable the church in Africa to unleash its own potential in the response to HIV and AIDS. Churches in Europe and North America should continue to provide resources to the church in Africa as it strives to run its programmes. However, their input should not constitute the bulk of resources available to the church in Africa. As it endeavours to provide effective responses to HIV and AIDS, the church in Africa needs to utilize available resources and depend less on external funds.

Limited Experience in Fundraising, Monitoring and Evaluation

The church in Africa, at least since the 1990s, has shown a lot of passion to run projects. However, it has limited experience in the area of fundraising. One of the major issues that has emerged during workshops run by the Ecumenical HIV/AIDS Initiative in Africa (EHAIA) of the World Council of Churches (WCC) is the need for skills in project design and management. [65] Church leaders have consistently identified this as a clear need. They require further training to enable them to access local and external funds.

In those instances where churches have been able to access local and external funds, poor monitoring and evaluation have characterized many projects. The church is often motivated to 'get on with the job' and therefore struggles with documentation. Sometimes partners operating with the stereotype of Africans as corrupt assume that resources have been misappropriated, whereas in fact all that has happened is that the church has been 'too busy' implementing. Churches are not trained in record-keeping.

> The programmes are there but documentation is a problem. Donor requirements for project proposals, monitoring, evaluation and reports can be extremely onerous and time consuming. FBOs are largely implementers: they are the 'doers'. Few are trained to meet the documentation requirements of major funding agents. [66]

The church in Africa urgently requires capacity building to make it more effective in mobilizing and utilizing resources in contexts of HIV. It should not leave monitoring and evaluation to the Holy Spirit.[67] In its quest to become AIDS

---

[65] See, for example, Prisca Mokgadi, 'Project Design and Management', in Dube, *HIV/AIDS and the Curriculum*, pp. 143–51.

[66] Parry, *Responses*, p. 17.

[67] A comment made during a session at the PACANET Pre-ICASA Conference, Abuja, Nigeria, 3 December 2005.

competent, the church in Africa must take its stewardship role seriously. It must ensure that the resources that it finds are used effectively. James R. Cochrane, a South African scholar, observes:

> That there is a great deal of money floating around to do more than is being done, particularly as regards HIV and AIDS, reflects in part an inability to use that money effectively, efficiently and ethically. This is true within the circles of the church as much as anywhere. Among the greatest burdens for ordinary people working for health out of faith-based organizations and initiatives or congregations is management of finance and funds.[68]

The magnitude of the HIV challenge means that the church in Africa must overcome its limitations in project planning, monitoring and evaluation. As the need continues to increase, especially in relation to orphans and other vulnerable children, it will require expertise in fundraising. As more resources become available in the wake of HIV, the need to adopt a more professional approach to financial management has never been greater. This will enhance the church's capacity to stem the tide of HIV in Africa.

---

[68] James R. Cochrane, 'Of Bodies, Barriers, Boundaries and Bridges: Ecclesial Practice in the Face of HIV and AIDS', *Journal of Theology for Southern Africa* 126, 2006, p. 23.

Chapter 3
Churches With Friendly Feet

African churches need to be welcoming if they are to accompany people living with HIV. Very few churches in Africa have succeeded in providing hospitable space to those of us living with HIV. In most instances, the preaching continues to engender stigma and discrimination. Over a quarter of century into the epidemic, many preachers continue to mock people with AIDS. As Canon Gideon Byamugisha, an Anglican priest from Uganda openly living with HIV has said, such preachers want to use AIDS to control the church. Instead, they should be using the church to control AIDS. [69] Messages that seek to scare people have proven to be ineffective.

Churches that are open, warm and welcoming are a key resource in the response to the epidemic. Welcoming churches enable people living with HIV to openly share their stories. The challenge of disclosure is otherwise a daunting one. Due to the factors associated with theological rigidity, the church is often regarded as an unsafe place for people to disclose their HIV status. Radikobo Ntsimane, a South African scholar, cites one respondent who declared, 'The church is the last place I would disclose my status.'[70] A woman in Swaziland living with HIV expressed her reservations with the church in this way: 'when it comes to AIDS, the church suffers from a failure to love. It is an insensitive and judgmental institution that alienates people living with HIV.'[71]

Particularly during the early phase of the epidemic (1980 to the early 1990s), the church in Africa (and elsewhere) tended to categorize HIV and AIDS as the 'sinner's disease'. In the minds of most Christians, HIV was a 'worldly' issue, affecting individuals and communities that operated out-

---

[69] Gideon Byamugisha at the World Council of Churches' Ninth Assembly in Porto Alegre, Brazil, 14–23 February 2006.

[70] Radikobo Ntsimane, 'To Disclose or Not to Disclose: An Appraisal of the Memory Box Project as a Safe Space for Disclosure of HIV Positive Status', *Journal of Theology for Southern Africa* 125, 2006, p. 14.

[71] Mercy Dlamini (not her real name) at the Ecumenical HIV/AIDS Initiative in Africa (EHAIA), Theologians' Workshop on Culture, Gender, Sexuality and HIV and AIDS, Ezulwuni, Swaziland, 19–22 June 2006.

side the demands of the gospel. The Deuteronomistic view
of God rewarding good and punishing evil tended to pre-
dominate. It was reinforced by the interpretation of health
and well-being in African cultures. Disease has been associated with wrong-doing in African Traditional Religions.[72]
The combination of selective biblical and traditional interpretations allowed the church in Africa to classify HIV as
an external problem that had no bearing on its theology
and practice.

As noted earlier, in many places the pulpit became the
command centre for propagating messages that added to
the pain of members of the body of Christ living with HIV.
Some dramatic preachers imitated the difficulties that some
among us with AIDS have in walking, to much laughter
from the congregation. The intention was to shake believers out of their complacency. Unfortunately, the assumption that AIDS was only an issue 'for those out there' was
wrong.

As already indicated, by remaining insensitive to those
of us living with HIV, the church has been effectively reinforcing an us and them attitude. This unfortunate development led to the silence and withdrawal from the church of
many among us living with HIV. The church needs to be a
welcoming community. In its liturgy, it must acknowledge
and reflect the presence of those of us living with HIV. This
could be by way of special services, granting space for the
testimonies of the infected and affected and ensuring local
congregations observe key dates like World AIDS Day.[73]

Developing and Upholding HIV and AIDS Policies

It is crucial that churches develop and adopt HIV and
AIDS policies. This is an important step towards becoming a welcoming church. Although experience has shown
that policies might easily become glorified pieces of paper

[72] See Laurenti Magesa, *African Religion: The Moral Traditions of Abundant Life*, Nairobi, Paulines Publications Africa, 1998, pp. 156–9.
[73] Musa W. Dube, ed., *Africa Praying: A Handbook on HIV/AIDS Sensitive Sermon Guidelines and Liturgy*, Geneva, World Council of Churches,
2003.

40

that do not guide action, developing a policy demonstrates a church's commitment to respond effectively to HIV and AIDS. A good example is the Catholic Church in Zimbabwe, which provided the reflection *Forward in Hope: A Plan of Action for the Next Twelve Months*. The plan was developed in January 2005 in partnership with EHAIA. Under the title 'People living with HIV/AIDS' (PLWHA), the following is noted:

> We shall encourage more parishes to form support groups where PLWHA and those affected feel safe and accepted.
> A change of attitudes and beliefs is required in many of our parishes. We recommend, therefore, that time be given in the meetings of existing parish groups to present accurate information and thoughtful spiritual reflection concerning the varied aspects of HIV/AIDS.
> Using our existing structures we can work towards a truly consistent Christian response with regard to care, compassion and holistic support.
> We will encourage all who are responsible for homilies, liturgies and prayers to be sensitive in their choice of words and texts so that issues surrounding HIV/AIDS can be creatively introduced and explored.
> Look for opportunities to invite people living with HIV/AIDS to speak at our parish functions so as to share their experience and increase our understanding. [74]

The issues raised in this plan of action demonstrate the church's awareness of the challenges that those of us living with HIV face inside the church. Welcoming churches ensure that those among us living with HIV feature prominently in the life of the church. Such churches recognize that church members living with HIV do not belong to the margins of the church. If the church is to live up to the expected standard of being a home to all, it should warmly embrace those of us living with HIV. It must recognize that one's HIV status is not a barrier to fellowship in the body of Christ.

[74] *Forward in Hope: A Plan of Action for the Next Twelve Months – A Response to HIV/AIDS By the Joint Conference of Major Religions Superiors of Zimbabwe*, Harare, Health Desk, CMRS/CMWRS, 2005.

We need to guard against creating a 'special wing' for those of us living with HIV within congregations. While it is clear that those of us who are living with HIV need space for sharing experiences, we need to 'mainstream' HIV in the life of the church. The concept of Greater/Meaningful Involvement of People with AIDS (G/MIPA) is instructive in this regard. Welcoming churches ensure the meaningful involvement of those of us living with HIV in Sunday Schools, and in youth, women's and men's groups. They do not simply make token concessions to those of us living with HIV. Instead, in word and deed, they live out the reality of the church living with HIV.

Inclusive Communities

Welcoming churches are by definition inclusive communities. They interpret their mission in the manner of Jesus, who embraced the marginalized. They live up to the definition of what it means to be Christian – imitators of Christ. Such churches are oozing with love and acceptance. They do not dwell on what they do not have, such as massive financial resources and quality medication. In the manner of Peter at the gate of the temple (Acts 3:6), they give what they have: abundant love. Thus:

> There have been considerable amounts of literature focusing on the Christian responses to HIV/AIDS on the Internet, in Christian theological seminaries and in libraries, and the weight has been placed on looking for external resolutions. Ineffective policies and support programmes, lack of resources and funding, albeit important considerations, have been highlighted and a simple united Christian response has been overlooked – not one culminating from a collection of theological doctrines but one that is simply Christian. All Christians are equipped to bring to those in need the Christian spirit of giving: emotional strength, the assurance of love from God, biblical study and prayer, friendship and love. [75]

---

[75] *Churches and HIV/AIDS: A Research on KwaZulu–Natal Christian Council (KZNCC) Member Church Initiatives and Strategies in Response to the HIV/AIDS Crisis in KZN: Draft Report*, Pietermaritzburg, KwaZulu–Natal Church AIDS Network (KZNCAN), May 2005, p. 10.

In a sense, 'welcoming churches' is a tautology. The very idea of 'welcoming' is integral to being church. A church cannot be a church if it is not welcoming. Being open, inclusive and hospitable is at the very heart of what it means to be church. When a body of believers engages in actions and practices that alienate those of us living with HIV, it ceases to be worthy of the label 'church'. For a church necessarily creates a safe haven to those who carry heavy loads, following Jesus' invitation (Matthew 11:28).

African churches are compelled to become welcoming and loving churches in the era of HIV. The exhortation to love one another (1 John 4:7) becomes central in the context of HIV. Love engenders solidarity and banishes stigma. Love compels embracing people living with and affected by HIV and AIDS. Love ceases being an abstract concept when it is lodged in the hearts of believers. It propels them into action. They embrace those of us living with HIV. They open their hearts, homes and churches to people affected by HIV. Love erases the artificial separation between 'us' and 'them'. Loving churches have had the realization, nay revelation, that the church is living with HIV.

Welcoming churches are particularly sensitive to the needs of orphans and other vulnerable children in the wake of HIV. The number of orphans in most parts of Southern Africa is staggering: 'In Sub-Saharan Africa, AIDS had orphaned 12 million children by 2003; by 2010, 18 million children are expected to be orphaned by AIDS.'[76] The church has been actively involved in responding to the needs of orphans and vulnerable children. It has endeavoured to be friendly towards children. Following her exposition of Mark 9:33–37 and Mark 10:13–16 in which she highlights Jesus' positive attitude to children, Musa Dube writes:

> It seems that we need to revalue what Jesus said in our search for an action-oriented theology of children's rights. We need to note that his answer to a group of his male disciples who were arguing who is great, was to bring a child to them and commend

---

[76] Peter R. Lamptey, Jami L. Johnson and Marya Khan, 'The Global Challenge of HIV and AIDS', *Population Bulletin* 61, 1, 2006, p. 6.

them to welcome/care for a child – a role that is normally associated with women. Yet one cannot overemphasize the importance of getting men involved in giving quality care to children
and in the fight against HIV/AIDS in general.[77]

Dube's insights are important as the church in Africa strives
to ensure that it provides safe space for children. Jesus demonstrated that children deserve to be treated with respect.
As Dube argues, the church in Africa needs to uphold the
rights of children. Critically, men should begin to play a
more prominent role in giving quality care to children. The
HIV epidemic challenges the church in Africa to mobilize
men to follow the example of Jesus and prioritize children's
welfare. Welcoming churches expose the abuse of children
within homes, churches, schools and other institutions. As
we will see below, they utilize the positive attitude towards
children in both Christianity and African culture to protect
and nurture children. Churches that welcome children in
the era of HIV encourage a rereading of the Bible from the
point of view of children. They are aware that adult-centred
interpretations of the Bible are limited.[78]

Resurrecting Dead Spirits: Proclaiming Life
in Contexts of HIV and AIDS

As the church in Africa accompanies those of us living
with HIV and AIDS, it must proclaim life amid so much
death and devastation. The death of young, economically
productive people has sapped life out of many communities
in Sub-Saharan Africa. Many pupils in primary school have
attended the funerals of their schoolmates. On some occasions, wives and husbands have been buried within days
of each other. Some parents walk past the graves of their
children on their way to the fields. Death has rolled out a
mat and has made itself comfortable in many communities
in Southern Africa. How can one escape death's tentacles

---

[77] Musa W. Dube, 'Fighting with God: Children and HIV/AIDS in
Botswana', *Journal of Theology for Southern Africa* 114, 2002, p. 41.

[78] Gunnar Stalsett, 'Life Enhancing Potential', *Contact: A Publication of
the Health and Healing Programme*, WCC, 179, 2005, p. 35.

when coffin vendors patrol some high-density areas and the death industry booms?[79]

Heart-rending, mind-numbing and faith-shaking scenes are replayed many times across the region. Here, three children below the age of twelve bang themselves against the wall as their mother's coffin is taken out. There, a father cries uncontrollably as his daughter's body arrives from the mortuary. Behind the street, husband and wife hold hands and look away as their child's coffin is brought home before the final journey. Not too far away, a mother puts her hands at the back of her head. For the third time this year, she has viewed the body of her dead child. Like Rachel weeping ceaselessly for her children, she refuses to be consoled (Matthew 2:18).[80]

The sting of death plunges itself mercilessly into communities. Where funeral cars used to travel at a respectful speed, now they overtake *matatus*/kombis – a notable feat on its own. Tired mourners crack jokes as they seek to defy death. Exhausted women from the Mothers Union concede space to traditional drummers who invite mourners to dance as they mock death. Spontaneous ecumenism emerges as mourners see the practical benefit of singing popular funeral hymns and choruses. Performing denominational favourites would instigate a latter-day Babel experience, since many burials take place simultaneously in the urban cemetery. They cannot delay, for other convoys are waiting their turn. The earth is truly one massive, insatiable stomach!

With so much death around, the HIV epidemic has led to hopelessness and despair among many young people in Southern Africa. Some comment that they were 'born at the wrong time'.[81] They have watched many of their friends

---

[79] See Ezra Chitando, 'Survival Knows No Bounds: A Study of the Participation of Blacks in the Death Industry in Harare', *Journal for the Study of Religion* 12, 1 & 2, 1999, pp. 65–78.

[80] Musa W. Dube, 'In the Circle of Life: African Women Theologians' Engagement with HIV and AIDS', Consultancy Report Submitted to EHAIA, Harare, 2006, p. 2.

[81] Ezra Chitando, 'The Predicament of Zimbabwe's Post Independence Generation: Can the Church Offer Solutions?' *Journal of Black Theology in South Africa* 12, 2, 1998, p. 36.

fall sick and die. They have lost faith in the human project. While their contemporaries in Europe and North America can engage in youthful dreams, their own future threatens to be one long nightmare.

AIDS has killed at two, equally lethal levels. The first level is the physical death described above. It has left a broken landscape in Africa. [82] The second level is the killing of the future and the paralysis of the present. The epidemic has had the effect of demoralizing individuals and whole communities. It has blotted out dreams of a prosperous future, for the reality of dying young weighs on people. Both these forms of death are tragic.

The church has been accompanying families and communities in their encounters with death. Most pastors have admitted their exhaustion in conducting so many funerals. They have invested physical, spiritual and emotional resources to bury the dead. They spend more time at the graveyard than in the river of life. It is women's and youth groups that have taken the lead in consoling bereaved families. They lead in prayers and singing. Amid the desperation and desolation, the church maintains a comforting presence. On many occasions, I have attended funerals where preachers have sought to revive the spirits of mourners. The Bible provides words of healing and comfort. However, as we shall see below, there is a tendency to normalize death. How can the death of so many people be normal? How can it be the will of God that some children are born with HIV when parent-to-child transmission is now preventable?

A form-critical analysis of the funeral and memorial services that I have attended in Zimbabwe shows that Job 14:1–2 is quite popular. It reads, 'Man that is born of a woman is of few days, and full of trouble. He comes forth like a flower, and withers; he flees like a shadow, and continues not.' Preachers have proceeded to explain the high death rate in terms of human life being short by divine

---

[82] See the challenging photographs in Gideon Mendel, *A Broken Landscape: HIV and AIDS in Africa*, London, Network of Photographers in association with Action Aid, 2001.

design. Hearers of the Word are left convinced that the short life-span caused by AIDS in Africa is consistent with the plan of God.

Normalizing the Abnormal: Theologies of Death

A theology of death has tended to dominate in contexts of HIV and AIDS in Africa. Funeral hymns and choruses are being composed regularly. At one level, they belong to the theological category of lament.[83] This is justified as individuals and communities beseech God in the context of pain and death. However, in many instances, death is granted the final word. Death is embraced as the will of God. Sermons and songs are replete with messages of death. They condition congregations to accept abnormalities such as the death of so many young people. It is relatively easy for a theology of death to set in, as most people's lives are affected by it. Ministers and pastors are particularly vulnerable. Their lives are saturated with death. They spend most of their time burying the dead, counselling the bereaved or officiating at memorial services. In such a context, death weighs heavily on the consciousness of communities. It is easy to succumb to hopelessness and despair.[84]

The popularity of the 'Crying Song' in South Africa and Zimbabwe in 2006 and 2007 indicates this preoccupation with death. The Crying Song is an instrumental piece that conveys the sound of mourning. That such a song could gain popularity is indicative of the extent to which communities in Southern Africa are saturated with mourning. The song received extensive airplay on radio stations, public transport and night clubs. It testifies to the devastation caused by AIDS in the region. The song highlights the internalization of death by communities. Cries of agony and pain have become their daily bread.

---

[83] Maria Cimperman, *When God's People Have HIV/AIDS: An Approach to Ethics*, Maryknoll, NY, Orbis Books, 2005, pp. 26–7.

[84] I am indebted to participants at the Southern African Missiological Society Annual Congress, 'Mission as Creative and Holistic Action in Africa', 17 January 2007, University of Pretoria, for this paragraph. They were responding to my presentation, 'Poverty, Development and HIV and AIDS in Theological Learning'.

Questioning Death: Theologies of Life

A theology of life seeks to reanimate paralysed communities. AIDS competent churches in Africa are being called upon to energize communities to leave the valley of shadow of death and ascend the mountain of life and hope. They must leave the cemeteries and compose new songs of joy and hope. Where those without faith see doom and desolation, those with the eyes of faith must detect restoration and new life. Theologies of life breathe life into broken hearts. They are built on the conviction that the biblical stories of creation demonstrate God's decisive identification with life ahead of destruction and chaos.

It must be underscored that theologies of life need not be quick-fix, escapist strategies to cope with the high death rate. The raw pain and loss of meaning needs to be acknowledged. Humility and realism should be the basis of such a theology. Triumphalism should not be allowed to wish away the cries of agony that reverberate in so many African communities. Theologies of life are not built on an imaginary escape from death. Rather, they take death into account, but use it as a point of departure. They are a refusal to grant death the final word.

Celebrating Life: African Cultural Resources [85]

Theologies of life are consistent with African traditional approaches to death and life. [86] African beliefs and practices are a celebration of life. Life is good and must be enjoyed to the full. The anthropological beliefs in African Traditional Religions are predicated on the understanding that death is a fundamental human problem. The death of young people is regarded as a crisis that requires an urgent resolution. Life must be enhanced and celebrated. Traditional Africans

---

[85] I am indebted to Musa W. Dube for regarding African Traditional Religions as a resource in the African churches' response to HIV. Debates and discussions in the writing of the 'Theological Education by Extension HIV and AIDS Module on African Indigenous Religions' in Gaborone in July 2005 have informed this section.

[86] For an analysis of one specific African ethnic group, see Herbert Aschwanden, *Symbols of Life: An Analysis of the Consciousness of the Karanga*, Gweru, Mambo Press, 1983.

are stubbornly earthbound; that is, they are not preoccupied with the idea of a world to come. Life on earth should be experienced as a gift from God and the ancestors. Africans are not in a hurry to leave the world, as it is seen as a good place to be.

The reality of HIV shakes traditional African anthropological and soteriological beliefs to the core. The dominant belief is that one should live to a ripe old age. Dying young constitutes a fundamental human problem. It is a sign that relations between the dead and the living are strained. The services of a traditional healer may be sought, who may prescribe ritual action to prevent further deaths in the family. Death is an enemy that must be fought vigorously, which accounts for the use of protective charms and amulets. Forces that promote death, for example witchcraft, are actively resisted.

African ideas relating to salvation also demonstrate a preoccupation with longevity and abundance in the physical life. Tukunbo Adeyemo, an Evangelical African theologian, observes that salvation in African tradition focuses on success in worldly pursuits and is not world-negating.[87] Simon S. Maimela, a South African black theologian, maintains that salvation in African Traditional Religions is connected with prosperity in this life.[88] Death is seen as a negative force that upsets the life of the community. Traditional African beliefs and practices promote a pro-life agenda.

Although funerals are characterized by a lot of wailing and pain, steps are taken to remind mourners that death does not have the last word. In many African communities a fire or light is set in the room where the body lies. This symbolizes the continuity of life. In other communities, daughters-in-law dramatize the activities of the deceased. For example, if a man had been a schoolteacher, they may put on his clothes, take a piece of chalk and re-enact what he used to do. Others will sing and dance, taunting death

---

[87] Tukunbo Adeyemo, *Salvation in African Tradition*, Nairobi, Evangel Publishing House, 1979.

[88] Simon S. Maimela, 'Salvation in African Traditional Religions', *Missionalia* 13, 2, 1985, pp. 63–77.

and praising life. In traditional philosophy, life triumphs over death.

The language employed to refer to death is also consistent with the pro-life agenda. Euphemisms are used to promote a less devastating image. Among the Shona, it is said that the deceased wafamba (has travelled) and therefore will return. Different African languages underscore the belief that death is only temporary. Life, even though it might be experienced in a different form, wins the day. It is life that is acknowledged and emphasized. Death is an aberration that must be addressed urgently. African Traditional Religions therefore seek to promote life and undermine death.

While some religions are world-denying or world-negating, African Traditional Religions are world-affirming. For them, the world is not an evil place that deserves to be destroyed. Neither do they view human existence as a burden that must be endured. Human life and the created order should be nurtured. A celebration of life underpins the traditional worldview. Granted, there have been wars, gender injustice and other life-denying practices in the history of Africa, but they have not dampened the enthusiasm for life lived within space and time.

The interest in human life on this earth that runs through African Traditional Religions should become a strategic resource for the African churches on the journey towards AIDS competence. By focusing on the primacy and quality of life, African Traditional Religions have a positive attitude towards human earthly existence. By frustrating the ideal of living up to a ripe old age, AIDS strikes a blow to the indigenous understanding of life. African Traditional Religions provide useful resources for the development of African Christian theologies of life in contexts of HIV. There are helpful insights from African Traditional Religions that may be appropriated in the formulation of theologies of life.

First, African Traditional Religions regard death, especially that of young people, as a fundamental human problem. In most parts of Southern Africa, AIDS has become the leading cause of death within the economically active age group. While a theology of death seeks to normalize such a trend, a theology of life informed by indigenous interpretations of death problematizes it. A theology of life raises alarm and laments whenever death seeks permanent residence status within African communities.

Second, the focus on quality of life in African Traditional Religions might serve as a check on an unhealthy fixation with heaven and future bliss. A theology of life recognizes the tension between the 'now' and the 'not yet'. While a futuristic eschatology is an integral part of the Christian faith, in contexts of HIV it can easily sponsor or anchor theologies of death. The concern with health and well-being in African Traditional Religions finds resonance in the ministry of Jesus. Jesus was determined to ameliorate human suffering. Thus, 'Jesus also promoted life by fighting whatever diminishes it, such as disease, physical challenge, social exclusion, national oppression and hunger.'[89]

Third, African Traditional Religions swing into action whenever life-threatening forces besiege individuals, families or the community. This sense of urgency needs to be appropriated in African Christian theologies in contexts of HIV. Following the example of African traditionalists who seek the services of sacred practitioners and effect rituals to ward off dangers, African churches need to be proactive in meeting the needs of people living with HIV or AIDS. Theologies of life need to integrate access to life-enhancing drugs. Churches are required to play a leading role in ensuring that people living with HIV in Africa access antiretroviral drugs. Indigenous approaches to restoring health and well-being should inform the churches' urgency in responding to HIV.

It is important to adopt a more balanced approach to African cultures in contexts of HIV and to utilize the insights and practices of African cultures in the overall response to HIV. Musa Dube, for instance, has illustrated how divina-

---

[89] Moji A. Ruele, 'Facing the Challenge of HIV/AIDS in Southern Africa: Towards a Theology of Life', in Dube, *HIV/AIDS and the Curriculum*, p. 81.

tion and prophecy in African Traditional Religions can be
harnessed in HIV discourses.[90]

Churches with Warm Hearts: Theologies of Compassion

We have seen how the celebration of life in African
Traditional Religions can be utilized in the formulation of
African Christian theologies of life in contexts of HIV. It is
also crucial for churches in Africa to live out theologies of
compassion.

AIDS competent churches in Africa are necessarily compassionate churches. Too often, the term *compassion* evokes
notions of feeling pity for people in difficult circumstances.
It engenders the idea of one who is in a better position
feeling sorry for others who are worse off. Such a reading
of compassion tends to be patronizing. A compassionate
church does not feel sorry for those of us living with HIV.
Rather, it stands in solidarity with us. Theologies of compassion ensure that African churches are constantly reminded
that compassion is at the very heart of mission.

Joseph Huber tells us that the word *compassion* is derived
from Latin *compassus* and means 'suffering with another'.[91]
It implies the ability to identify with the journey of another.
In the phenomenology of religion, which is an approach
to the study of religion, the process of 'empathetic interpolation' is highly recommended.[92] It implies *feeling with*
the other person. Empathetic interpolation, or compassion,
means viewing the world as it is seen through the eyes of
the other. Compassion calls for putting on the shoes of the
other to feel where it hurts.

---

[90] Musa W. Dube, 'Adinkra! Four Hearts Joined Together: On Becoming
Healing-Teachers of African Indigenous Religion/s in HIV & AIDS Pre-
vention', in Isabel Apawo Phiri and Sarojini Nadar, eds, *African Women,
Religion, and Health: Essays in Honor of Mercy Amba Ewudziwa Oduyoye*,
Maryknoll, NY, Orbis Books, 2006, pp. 131–56.

[91] Joseph Huber, *Clusters of Grapes: Sow a Character and You Reap Des-
tiny*, Gweru, Mambo Press, 1984, p. 64.

[92] For a useful description of this approach, see James L. Cox, *Express-
ing the Sacred: An Introduction to the Phenomenology of Religion*, Harare,
University of Zimbabwe Publications, 1992.

Compassion compels churches in Africa to shun indifference in the face of HIV. 'Business as usual' becomes impossible when churches are *moved* with compassion. The notion of being moved is of utmost significance. Compassionate churches cannot sit still in the face of the suffering caused by HIV. Compassion should translate into concrete action that seeks to mitigate and eventually remove the pain caused by HIV and AIDS. Churches with warm hearts should also be churches with quick feet. They must act swiftly in their responses to pain in the face of HIV.

African churches that have been moved by compassion do not remain indifferent. Groups for children, youth, women and men are moved to go out and into action. Church leaders move their bodies to the homes of those of us with HIV. They are moved into practical activities that demonstrate love, acceptance and solidarity. They also move their tongues and speak out against stigma and discrimination.

There is a critical shortage of compassion in the world, among individuals, families and communities and nationally and internationally. Interpersonal relations are often characterized by indifference, if not outright hostility. The wars that break out in different parts of the world are largely due to the absence of compassion. Huber describes the contemporary world in this way:

> It is rather difficult to prick men's [sic] consciences in these blasé days. There is so much misery in the world, so you turn away! A little more won't make any difference. 'One cannot weep for the entire world', you can hear people saying. 'When you live next to a cemetery, you cannot weep for everyone', others say. The cynics say, 'No man limps because another is hurt.' [93]

There is so much cynicism in the world. The sense of community, of having a shared humanity, has been undermined. The reality of HIV in Africa can give rise to resignation. When millions have died and are dying, how does one hope to make a difference? How can one claim to be engaged in efforts to counter the effects of HIV when the battle appears

---

[93] Huber, *Clusters of Grapes*, p. 64.

to be a lost one, even before it has been fought? Is it even possible to be compassionate, or are we driven only by our selfish motives?

It is in a world with a critical deficiency of compassion that churches are expected to be awash with compassion. The HIV epidemic demands that churches in Africa become paragons of compassion. Indeed, as the salt of the earth, churches should be reservoirs of compassion even when it has dried up everywhere else. Compassionate churches make a difference by standing shoulder to shoulder with those of us with HIV. They regard the struggle as one struggle for full, abundant life for all human beings, created by God, in the image of God.

Churches in Africa are called to be compassionate because God is compassionate. Throughout the biblical text, God shows compassion to individuals, families, communities and nations. God's justice never cancels out God's compassion. The Hebrew Bible narrates how God demonstrates compassion towards the people of Israel, as well as other nations and individuals. God does not routinely punish human failure to attain ideal moral standards. Instead, God shows love and compassion towards humans and the entire created order. The Hebrew Bible highlights how God's compassion triumphs over retribution. It is compassion that lays the foundation for reconciliation and restoration. Furthermore, God has a special concern for widows, orphans and refugees. God shows compassion for them and seeks to change their circumstances.

The New Testament carries forward the idea of a compassionate God. The drama of salvation history (John 3:16) is predicated on compassion. God reaches out to humanity to counter estrangement. The ministry of Jesus was a vivid demonstration of compassion. Jesus was never indifferent to human distress. He was always propelled into action upon encountering human suffering. His miracles ensued from the compassion that he felt towards fellow human beings in extremely difficult circumstances. He was compassionate towards individuals and groups that counted for nothing or very little.

It is important to note that the compassion of Jesus does not lie in feeling sorry for the marginalized. His compassion is revolutionary and subversive. He challenges his society to become more compassionate, not by promising the most vulnerable that their reward will be in heaven but by acting decisively to restore their full human dignity in this life. Zambian church leader and theologian Japhet Ndhlovu has reflected on this theme:

> As the biblical teaching of the New Testament shows, the presence of God was not for the powerful and wealthy, first of all. The sinners and the prostitutes, the poor and the marginalized would be welcomed first. By identifying with these, by eating and drinking with them, Jesus overturned the accepted canons of religious and political respectability. It was eventually to cost him his life, as he was considered too subversive of the established order. After a show trial he was crucified outside the gates of the city, Jerusalem. For Christians who feel the urge to reject, avoid or neglect people living with HIV and AIDS, the counter-example of Jesus should be a forceful reminder, saying: 'As you do to one of these least ones …'[94]

The last phrase in Ndhlovu's reflection refers of course to the words of Jesus in Matthew 25:31–46, where Jesus defines commitment to him in terms of practical acts of compassion. Those who will enter the kingdom of God are not the most pious. Neither are they the ones who bellowed fiery sermons. Instead, those who have been *moved* by compassion and have fed the hungry, given water to the thirsty, accommodated strangers, clothed the naked, attended to the sick and visited prisoners stand to enter the kingdom. Jesus makes it abundantly clear that compassion is at the core of what it means to be his follower.

Compassionate churches in Africa in the era of HIV are obliged to attend to the needs of orphans and other vulnerable children. By meeting such needs as food, shelter and education, churches will be demonstrating their obedi-

---

[94] Japhet Ndhlovu, 'Zambia: The Compassion of God: A Relevant Theology in a Time of AIDS', in Elizabeth Knox-Seith, ed., *One Body: North–South Reflections in the Face of HIV and AIDS*, Copenhagen, Nordic-Foccisa Church Cooperation, 2005, p. 60.

ence to Christ. By reaching out to widows and widowers, orphans and grandparents, and others affected by HIV, African churches will be living up to the ideal of true religion (James 1:27). Compassion does not remain at the bottom of the believer's heart: it is translated into transformative action in response to HIV.

Chapter three pointed out that the church in Africa has a legacy of compassion. However, the HIV epidemic forced the church into a protective shell, especially in the 1980s and early 1990s. Although some pastors in some congregations demonstrated compassion towards those of us with HIV, on the whole the church was indifferent or hostile. How could it be compassionate towards those of us who 'were facing the full wrath of God'? Such theological rigidity prevented the church from unleashing waves of compassion, as directed by its founder.

Our compassion should not be restricted to those groups described as 'acceptable' by the church. Many Christians would happily be compassionate towards children who are born HIV positive. They would also search deep within themselves for compassion towards orphans. Similarly, they may feel that grandparents who look after orphaned children also deserve their compassion. However, they find it hard to feel compassion for sex workers, homosexuals, drug users and others. They might demand the conversion of individuals whose lifestyles are considered problematic. Only then would they consider being compassionate towards them. Such an attitude fails to recognize the revolutionary nature of Jesus' compassion.

The HIV epidemic vividly demonstrates the challenges of human relations. Compassion is also inextricably interwoven with this issue. HIV is a *relational* issue. Whether or not churches, governments, pharmaceutical companies and others provide medicines depends on their levels of compassion. When, how or whether we have sex is a relational matter. Compassion is required in all human dealings, particularly in the face of HIV.

Compassionate churches are a valuable resource in the overall response to HIV in Africa. Indeed, compassion is a characteristic that gives the church a comparative advantage. Without the variable of compassion, it would be difficult to distinguish churches from NGOs and government agencies, for example. It is compassion that underpins the churches' participation in programmes on HIV. They have distinctive competence in this particular domain, as their mission ensues from compassion. No one is considered too sick or too poor to be served by a true disciple of Christ. It is compassion that propels African Christian volunteers to seek out and assist those of us with HIV in the valleys and mountaintops.

'Nothing human is foreign to me': Compassion as a Human Trait

Of course, compassion is not the preserve of a particular religious tradition. [95] The humanistic motto 'Nothing human is foreign to me' was formulated on the understanding that it is possible for a human being to enter another human being's place of pain and to experience what that person feels. Each one of us is an autonomous human being but we share a common humanity. We experience pain, suffering, joy and all the emotions within a well-defined range. It is therefore possible for us to know how another person feels, for example, upon the loss of a loved one.

Ubuntu: Solidarity and Compassion in the Face of HIV and AIDS

The different religions in Africa converge in making compassion the key characteristic of believers. Genuine followers of religious precepts are defined and guided by compassion. In African Traditional Religions, God and the ancestors require that the community and individuals uphold the value of compassion. Compassion must be extended to all, including strangers. Society recognizes individuals who are compassionate in their dealings with

---

[95] See, for example, *Positive Muslims, HIV, AIDS and Islam: Reflections Based on Compassion, Responsibility and Justice*, Observatory, South Africa, Positive Muslims, 2004.

others. Laurenti Magesa, an African theologian, claims that while this rule might be transgressed, ideally one should uphold it:

> Instead, the behaviour that merits the praise of the community and showers upon one the blessings of the ancestors calls on a person to go out of the way to a neighbour's house next door to get water for a traveller if there is none in one's own house or to call out to passers-by to come and share a meal. These are the signs of a good, morally upright person. [96]

Ancestral blessings are assured for those who demonstrate compassion toward others. The concept of *Ubuntu* (common humanity) buttresses the idea of compassion in African Traditional Religions. [97] *Ubuntu* requires Africans to recognize and uphold the humanity of others. It is an appreciation of a shared identity. *Ubuntu* is an antidote to HIV and AIDS stigma and discrimination. If my being is dependent on your being, how can I lessen your dignity by shunning you? If I am tied to you, how can I seek to untie the knots? How can one *not* be moved by the suffering of those of us with HIV if we share a common human identity? *Ubuntu* provides a sound basis for compassion in African cultures.

The concept of *Ubuntu* is also significant in the struggle against discrimination based on race, sexuality, age, physical ability and other factors. [98] By reminding society that each one of us is connected to the other in intimate ways, *Ubuntu* challenges individualism and indifference. It provides a framework for solidarity and active compassion. Indeed, in African cultures, compassion towards individuals on the margins of society is promoted. One is expected to reach out towards orphans, the elderly and people with

---

[96] Magesa, *African Religion*, p. 156.

[97] See Augustine Shutte, *Ubuntu: An Ethic for the New South Africa*, Cape Town, Cluster Publications, 2001.

[98] See Joseph B. R. Gaie, 'Ethics of Breaking the Stigma: Biblical and Theological Perspectives', in Charles Klagba and C. B. Peter, eds, *Into the Sunshine: Integrating HIV/AIDS into the Ethics Curriculum*, Eloderet, Zapf Chancery, 2005, pp. 91–111.

disabilities. Acts of kindness toward such individuals are consistent with the values promoted by *Ubuntu*. Compassion empowers members of the human family to overcome all forms of discrimination.

The compassion that ensues from *Ubuntu* should equip African churches for the prophetic role in the era of HIV. If 'I am because you are', it follows that your pain is my pain. This chimes completely with Paul's analogy of the human body: 'If one member suffers, all suffer together' (1 Corinthians 12:26a). The solidarity that comes from sharing pain should motivate African churches to take their advocacy role seriously. How do I keep quiet when you, an extension of me, do not have access to antiretroviral drugs? How do I, a man, look away when you, a woman, are being raped and abused, when we share a common human identity? Can I, a father, remain silent when these orphans are harassed? What do silence, inaction and misaction do to my own humanity? [99]

Alongside this positive emphasis on compassion through Ubuntu, African cultures also highlight its importance by reminding individuals of the dire consequences of *not* showing compassion. Among the Shona people of Zimbabwe, for example, the concept of *ngozi* (avenging spirit) demonstrates the importance of compassion. It is believed that the spirit of a deceased individual who was not treated with compassion returns to cause suffering, misfortune and death in the family of the person who withheld compassion. Although the avenging spirit is usually associated with murder, it is believed to emerge from various cases of lack of compassion. For example, an avenging spirit could be that of an immigrant worker who was treated badly during his term of employment. Xenophobia, maltreatment of workers and unfair labour practices are some of the reasons why spirits of deceased foreigners are believed to return to haunt the living. Failure to provide assistance to travellers in difficult

---

[99] Gideon Byamugisha has drawn attention to the fact that often our *in*action (when we do nothing) and *mis*action (when our actions, despite our noble intentions, are harmful) have contributed to the spread of HIV.

circumstances is also believed to give rise to an avenging spirit. All these cases demonstrate that compassion is a key aspect of African Traditional Religions.

The emphasis on compassion within African cultures should motivate African Christians in contexts of HIV. Proverbs, folktales and myths play an important role in reinforcing teaching on compassion. The various African languages are full of proverbs that encourage members of the community to be compassionate towards one another. These proverbs are a rich reservoir for developing an African oral theology of compassion in the context of HIV. Folktales also seek to remind African audiences of the need to be sensitive to the struggles of others. Characters who show compassion succeed in their ventures, while those who are cruel or indifferent do not prosper.

African cultural resources are useful for developing a theology of compassion. The churches in Africa need to be creative in order to harness these resources in the struggle against HIV and AIDS stigma and discrimination. For example, the Shona have a proverb, *Chawana hama hachisekwi* (One does not rejoice when misfortune befalls a relative/another person). This proverb can be valuable in mobilizing communities to appreciate that the struggle of the 'other' is in fact the self's own struggle. To be indifferent to the challenges of fellow human beings is ultimately to deny one's own humanity. The proverb makes a passionate call for compassion and solidarity. It can be utilized to undermine HIV and AIDS stigma and discrimination.

Another Shona proverb captures the healing power of compassion: *Shungu neganyu zvinodzimba wotandadza, asi chido chinomusimbisa* (Grief and sighing hurt a person in agony, while loving compassion strengthens him). [100] Loving compassion has a positive impact on the health of the person in agony. Often, just being present makes all the difference to someone in pain. Compassion reaches where no medication reaches: the inner recesses of the human heart. Johan

---

[100] Huber, *Clusters of Grapes*, p. 65.

Viljoen, a person living with HIV, confirms the impact of 'the ministry of presence':

> By simply being there, we allow the Holy Spirit to work through us. When I was at my lowest point in the hospital, a nun whom I now know well came to visit me. I was too weak to communicate and I drifted in and out of consciousness. She sat next to my bed, without saying anything. She sat there for half an hour and then quietly got up and left. *This visit did more to strengthen and encourage me, than any intervention by the doctors.* [101]

Alongside the centrality of compassion to African cultures, the concept is also key to other religions found on the continent. A whole study would be required to do justice to the theme of compassion in world religions. All we need emphasize here is that compassion should translate into activism for the human rights of those of us living with and affected by HIV and AIDS. The world's religions have values that promote such human rights. [102] These values need to be harnessed in the struggle to ensure that people living with HIV and AIDS have access to life in all its fullness.

Finally, theologies of compassion for churches in Africa should not be mere intellectual formulations – no matter how important such formulations may be. Compassion compels and propels. Compassionate churches are at the forefront of designing and implementing programmes to address different aspects of HIV. They look after orphans and other vulnerable children. They stand for the rights of women in the face of stifling cultural practices. They press for access to life-prolonging drugs. They relieve grandparents who struggle to look after orphans with meagre resources. They are actively involved in home-based care.

---

[101] Johan Viljoen, 'Responsibility and Caring for One Another: Response to Paper by Sr Patricia Fresen', in Stuart C. Bate, ed., *Responsibility in a Time of AIDS: A Pastoral Response by Catholic Theologians and AIDS Activists in Southern Africa*, 2003, p. 71. Italics added.

[102] See Leroy S. Rouner, *Human Rights and the World's Religions*, Notre Dame, IN, University of Notre Dame Press, 1988.

Thousands of caregivers – almost all of them women! – are caring for thousands of patients. What do they do? It starts with washing the patient, doing household chores, looking for water and fuel, cooking food if there is any, giving advice on diets and training family members to care for the patient. It is very important to repeat over and over that one cannot get HIV/AIDS this way. To show that it is safe to touch and hug the patient. These caregivers do a lot to counteract the stigma which is still connected with the disease, even in countries like Uganda where the prevalence rates have declined. The ongoing counselling of client and family is of paramount importance in order to facilitate acceptance and positive living. Many caregivers prepare clients for death, including writing a will and helping them to think about the children they will leave behind.

The pastoral component of these programmes is obvious everywhere. I did not come across any home-based care programme in Africa affiliated with the church without communal prayer, where sharing the faith is not a very important feature of the care being given. [103]

Compassionate churches in Africa actively and deliberately mobilize men to participate in the provision of care to those among us with AIDS. [104] Women carry the burden of care in Africa. Home-based care programmes are in fact women-based care programmes. More men are needed to share this burden. Compassionate churches in Africa will be required to care for the carers, [105] who in most cases are women and girls. They need to support grandmothers who are starting all over in the parental role. Compassionate churches reach homes, institutions and centres where many people caring for those of us with AIDS trudge on against formidable odds.

Compassionate churches engage in *inreach*. They minister internally, recognizing that the church itself is in con-

[103] Raphaela Handler, 'Advocacy for Care/Access to Treatment', in Michael F. Czerny, ed., *AIDS and the African Church: To Shepherd the Church, Family of God in Africa, in the Age of AIDS*, Nairobi, Paulines Publications Africa, 2005, p. 21.

[104] This point is made in the second book of this series, *Acting in Hope*.

[105] Ricus Dullaert, ed., *Care for the Caregivers Manual*, Nijmegen, ICAN; Amsterdam, Het Spinhuis, 2006.

tinuous need of conversion. In times of HIV, believers need to be constantly reminded of the importance of compassion. They need to be challenged to show compassion toward individuals and groups within the human family. It is therefore critical that the liturgy of compassionate churches in Africa be creative and motivational. It must empower the people of God to be ambassadors whose works are characterized by compassion.

Musa Dube has formulated a moving and effective closing prayer and commissioning that should transform indifferent churches into compassionate armies in the face of HIV.

Closing: Responsive Prayer

Leader: Open our eyes Oh Lord,
All: So that we can all see you in the faces of those who suffer from HIV/AIDS.
Leader: Open our hearts,
All: So that we can feel the pains of all who suffer as your sorrow and suffering.
Leader: Open our ears,
All: So that we can hear the cry of the grieving as your cry.
Leader: Open our hands,
All: So that we can serve and feed the orphans, widows and people living with HIV/AIDS.
Leader: Open our feet,
All: So that we can go and be with those who are in home-based care.
Leader: Open our minds,
All: So we can become prophetic to social injustice that fuels HIV/AIDS.
Commissioning
Go with the God of compassion.
Go with Emmanuel, the God With Us.
Go with the Comforter to liberate creation from oppression.
Go and heal God's people and world. [106]

---

[106] Dube, 'Compassion', in Dube, *Africa Praying*, p. 101.

Chapter 4
Churches With Anointed Hands

Compassion is closely related to healing. As we saw, compassion can facilitate healing. Unfortunately, the concept of healing is highly controversial in contexts of HIV. In fact, critics charge that claims of miraculous spiritual/faith healing of those of us with HIV constitute one of the most retrogressive aspects of FBOs and churches in Africa. Others within the church maintain that fake divine healers have dealt lightly with the wound of God's people by proclaiming 'peace, peace' where these is no peace (Jeremiah 6:13–14). They assert that in the absence of a scientifically proven cure for HIV, all talk of healing and cure is at best misleading and at worst dangerous. The topic elicits diametrically opposed views that cut across denominational, theological, class, race, gender and other distinctions.

Healing has been a major concern of the World Council of Churches. Debate on healing and the church has been a contentious and divisive issue in the ecumenical movement. [107] It requires tact and sensitivity. Usually, the key theological question is whether healing that appears to defy the usual, known medical processes, healing that is *miraculous*, can happen. Post-Enlightenment advocates maintain that such healing does not occur; in those instances where it is believed to have occurred, independent, scientific verification should be sought. On the other hand, many Christians, especially in the South, are convinced that 'with God nothing will be impossible' (Luke 1:37). [108] They contend that healing that goes against established medical knowledge is possible and does happen. Other Christians are sceptical. They are critical of most claims of miraculous healing but remain open to its possibility.

It is against this backdrop that one might suggest that in most instances, controversy over healing is a result of dif-

---

[107] For a helpful overview, see Christoph Benn and Erlinda Sentarias, 'Health, Healing and Wholeness', in Claudia Sander, ed., *Neglected Dimensions in Health and Healing: Concepts and Explorations in an Ecumenical Perspective*, Study Document No. 3, Tubigen, German Institute for Medical Mission, 2001, pp. 8–27.

[108] Television advertisements by one Pentecostal ministry in Zimbabwe maintain that individuals are healed of AIDS because 'nothing is impossible with God'.

64

ferent interpretations of the concept. Narrow definitions of healing tend to be technical and limiting: healing is reduced to *curing*. Curing is only an aspect of healing, confined to the physical dimension. What is required is a more holistic understanding of healing, involving the physical, psychical, spiritual and other dimensions. [109]

Healing can take place in the absence of a cure. [110] If we understand healing in terms of restoration and reintegration, we can imagine how it is possible to be healed even if one has not been cured. A good example is how healing occurs when those of us with HIV no longer have to experience exclusion, stigma and discrimination. When those among us with HIV receive love and acceptance, healing occurs. Healing entails overcoming alienation and brokenness. It entails the idea of recreating a sense of belonging and community.

Researchers within the field of world religions have identified health and well-being as a universal preoccupation. [111] Religions promise their adherents health as one of life's greatest gifts. In the different religions of the world, the tendency to associate ill-health and suffering with punishment has been responsible for the interpretation of HIV as evidence of divine retribution. As a result, some people have been driven away from their own religions. [112] It is therefore crucial for theologies of healing in contexts of HIV to incorporate aspects of confession and reintegration. Churches must acknowledge, as some indeed have done, that theological rigidity has resulted in stigma and discrimination.

The church has always been engaged in different forms of healing. Medical missions were particularly important

[109] See Nico Koopman, 'Curing or Caring? Theological Comments on Healing', *Religion and Theology* 13, 1, 2006, p. 40, n. 4.

[110] Usha Jesudasan and Gert Ruppell, eds, *Healing as Empowerment: Discovering Grace in Community*, Geneva, World Council of Churches, n.d., p. 28.

[111] See Martin Prozesky, *Religion and Ultimate Well-Being*, London, Macmillan, 1984.

[112] Steven Lux and Kristine Greenaway, *Scaling Up Effective Partnerships: A Guide to Working with Faith-Based Organizations in the Response to HIV and AIDS*, Geneva, Ecumenical Advocacy Alliance, 2006, p. 6.

for the growth of Christianity in Africa. In many countries, the church owns a significant percentage of health facilities. Church-related institutions were also pioneers in providing care to those of us living with or affected by HIV or AIDS in most parts of Sub-Saharan Africa. However, there are also other forms of healing:

> The following count among the most usual forms of healing ministries in local congregations, hospitals or hospices:
> Intercession, private or public
> Laying on of hands
> Anointing with oil
> Reconciliation and absolution
> Healing the family tree
> Healing of memories
> Self-organized groups of people in need (self-help groups, e.g. Alcoholics Anonymous)
> Visiting the sick
> Praying groups for people with illnesses
> Counselling services
> Hospice centres and people accompanying the dying
> Prayers for deliverance from evil spirits (exorcism)
> It is important that each congregation recognizes and encourages the different gifts and talents related to those different forms of healing ministries in its own midst. [113]

Judging by this list of Dietrich Werner's, it is entirely legitimate to refer to healing in contexts of HIV, even if no cure is available right now. Prayer, laying on of hands, visiting the sick and counselling are vital components of the healing process. It is in prayer that churches provide a dimension that other NGOs do not possess. Given the importance of religion to African life, [114] it is vital that churches prioritize the healing ministry in the era of HIV.

Alongside its own healing ministry, the church in Africa is called upon to take up an advocacy role on behalf of poor

---

[113] Dietrich Werner, 'Appendix: Pastoral Guidelines on Healing Ministries in the Local Congregations and Health Services: 15 Key Points for Orientation', in Jesudasan and Ruppell, *Healing as Empowerment*, pp. 90–1.

[114] See Peter J. Paris, *The Spirituality of African Peoples: The Search for a Common Moral Discourse*, Minneapolis, MN, Fortress Press, 1995.

people living with HIV in Sub-Saharan Africa. With recent advances in antiretroviral drugs, HIV should no longer progress to AIDS, leading to death. The church must reclaim the definition of health and comprehensive well-being as key aspects of salvation to all. It must play a leading role in tackling impediments to the health of the poor in Africa. According to James R. Cochrane:

> A church that takes a preferential option for the health of the poor is a church faithful to the healing and wholeness implied by the Latin word salus, from which we derive 'salvation', or the Greek *soteria* and its Hebrew equivalent yesa, which variously mean healthy, safe, or 'free from limitations' through deliverance from factors that constrain or confine it. Redeeming life from that which threatens it, including disease in some uses in the Hebrew Bible, is the core meaning.[115]

Japhet Ndhlovu reinforces this idea of salvation as being inclusive of health and wholeness. According to Ndhlovu, the church needs to reclaim the vision of holistic healing. It should prophetically proclaim the connection between heath care and social justice. The church should uphold the biblical definition of health, healing and wholeness:

> God's intention for creation is expressed in the Old Testament vision of shalom: a term which indicated a wholeness, fulfilment, harmony and peace that characterized the earth and all its inhabitants. This is the root of the Bible's understanding of health; it provides a basis for the Old Testament understanding of salvation. This shalom is never individual but corporate, known in community.[116]

The New Testament carries forward the idea of healing. In the gospels, Jesus is presented as the healer *par excellence*. Whenever he encounters people with disability, he acts to restore health. Jesus heals lepers, the blind, the paralysed and many others. His ministry focuses on defeating ill-

---

[115] James R. Cochrane, 'Of Bodies, Barriers, Boundaries and Bridges: Ecclesial Practice in the Face of HIV and AIDS', *Journal of Theology for Southern Africa* 126, 2006, p. 18.

[116] Japhet Ndhlovu, 'Zambia: The Healing Church', in Knox-Seith, *One Body*, p. 31.

health. Jesus demonstrates love and compassion in the face of pain and suffering.

In as much as Jesus accomplishes the outstanding feat of physical healing, he plays an equally important role in healing relationships. Consequently, the sex worker and the tax collector who are rehabilitated by Jesus are as healed as the paralytic was healed. Jesus restores physical health and addresses broken relationships. He sides with the poor and the marginalized. He challenges oppressive structures that threaten the well-being of the majority. Jesus emerges as an individual who promotes social justice. His healing ministry is holistic and revolutionary. The church in Africa should seek to follow his model of healing in the face of HIV.

Healing in African Churches: Challenges in the Face of HIV

Healing remains one of the most attractive aspects of African Christianity. While most mainline churches have adopted the Western dichotomy of the physical and the spiritual and have thus left physical healing to biomedicine, AICs and Pentecostal/Charismatic churches continue to draw many people due to their healing ministries. However, the rise of charismatic healers like Archbishop Milingo[117] and Fr Nkwera testifies to the importance of healing to African Catholicism. In Ghana, for example, mainline churches are experiencing the full effects of the influence of Pentecostalism, with healing as one distinctive feature.[118]

The popularity of healing in many African churches is due to the centrality of healing in African cultures. Healing and prosperity are key concepts in African Traditional Religions.[119] The traditional healer/diviner/medicine wo/man is an important sacred practitioner who defeats illness

---

[117] Gerrie Ter Haar, *The Spirit of Africa: The Healing Ministry of Archbishop Milingo of Zambia*, London, Hurst, 1992.

[118] See Cephas N. Omenyo, 'From the Fringes to the Centre: Pentecostalization of the Mainline Churches in Ghana', *Exchange* 34, 1, 2005, pp. 39–60.

[119] Chirevo V. Kwenda, 'Affliction and Healing: Salvation in African Religion', *Journal of Theology for Southern Africa* 103, 1999, pp. 1–12.

68

and misfortune. She or he promotes health and well-being at the individual and community levels. Such individuals are believed to possess spiritual powers that qualify them to tackle any form of illness. In the contemporary period, some traditional healers have claimed to have healed some among us with HIV.

Many AICs have responded to the interest in healing among Africans. Although there were many reasons for the emergence of AICs, spiritual healing is among the more prominent. Mainline churches in Africa tended to overlook or dismiss African interpretations of sickness and health. They were too quick to dismiss the African concern with spiritual factors. They chose to concentrate on the physical. Across Sub-Saharan Africa, AICs emerged with an emphasis on healing through the power of the Holy Spirit.

Similarly, African Pentecostal churches rose to prominence in the 1990s. Like the AICs, they place emphasis on the role of the Holy Spirit. However, they differ from AICs in their proclamation of the gospel of prosperity. They focus on 'healing and deliverance', as well as 'health and wealth'. Combining North American teachings on prosperity and indigenous approaches to health, they maintain that true Christians are destined to health and prosperity. God is not poor. Christians are supposed to be in good health, physically and financially.

At crusades,[120] on posters and through other media, some Pentecostal preachers promise healing from *all* afflictions through the power of the Holy Spirit. Testimonies by people who claim to have been healed add weight to the promises made. With the firm conviction that with God all things are possible, some people with HIV have sought a reversal of their HIV status from such healers. People with cancer and other illnesses have also sought the services of charismatic healers.

---

[120] See, for example, Zacharia Wanakacha Samita, *Christian Crusades in Nairobi: An Analysis of Socio-Religious Factors Underlying their Upsurge*, Social Science Research Report Series No. 9, Addis Ababa, OSSREA, 1998.

In Southern Africa some prophets from AICs have also claimed to provide healing services to needy clients. In some instances, they have put up posters with full-sized photographs of the prophet and captions that inform potential clients that they can treat HIV. Paul Gundani, a Zimbabwean scholar, describes the advertisements of prophets in Harare:

> The posters and metal plates appeal to all who suffer from a myriad of physical, spiritual, social and psychic problems to come to the prophet for treatment and healing. These prophets claim to be able to treat patients suffering from all manner of illness caused by witchcraft and sorcery, chronic headaches, barrenness, impotence, stomach illness, sexually transmitted infections and a variety of cancers. Apart from these diseases the prophets also claim to be able to be responsible for a variety of misfortunes, ranging from unemployment, victimization at work, complicated pregnancy, family feuds and loss of property through burglary and theft. [121]

Pentecostal preacher-healers and AIC prophets are united in their conviction that the Holy Spirit defeats all illness, including HIV and AIDS. Healing crusades and healing cabins also attract members of mainline churches, Muslims and followers of other religions. In many instances, biomedicine is ridiculed as highly limited. There have been cases where some people taking antiretroviral drugs have been made to stop doing so after attending charismatic healing sessions. Sadly, there have also been cases of hypocrisy:

> My pastor has been preaching about the importance of faith. According to him, if one truly believes in the power of God, they should no longer trust drugs made by human hands. He has asked members of his congregation who are on antiretroviral drugs to discontinue. Prayer is more than enough, he said. However, when I went to collect my antiretroviral drugs last month, I met him. He had obviously come to collect his own antiretroviral drugs. I was so shocked that I have not attended any church service in the last three months. [122]

---

[121] Paul H. Gundani, 'Church Media, and Healing: A Case Study from Zimbabwe', *Word and World* 21, 2, 2001, p. 137.

[122] Mercy Dlamini (not her real name) at the Ecumenical HIV/AIDS Initiative in Africa (EHAIA) 'Theologians' Workshop on Culture, Gender, Sexuality and HIV and AIDS', Ezulwini, Swaziland, 19–22 June 2006.

70

Clearly, some preachers are not practising what they preach. While they encourage others to stop taking antiretroviral drugs, they continue to do so themselves. This raises the issue of sincerity. The church in Africa is regarded as a credible institution but when pastors act insincerely in this way, the church's credibility is compromised.

Claims that legitimate Christians do not endure ill-health and poverty are also theologically questionable. The gospel of prosperity can be quite appealing, especially in most African contexts characterized by extreme poverty. The sorry state of most health delivery systems leaves people with very little choice when they are promised free healing. Churches in Africa need to take seriously the pain of those of us living with HIV and AIDS and refrain from 'quick fix' solutions. By adopting healing and empowering approaches to HIV and AIDS, churches can become more effective. 'When we become aware that we do not have to escape our pains but that we can mobilize them into a common search for life, those very pains are transformed from expressions of despair into signs of hope.' [123]

An African Theology of Healing in the Era of HIV

There is an urgent need to develop an African theology of healing in contexts of HIV and AIDS.[124] Such a theology should synthesize the different therapeutic systems operating in most African countries: traditional healing, Christian faith healing and biomedicine. Such a theology would begin with the acknowledgement that God wills that all humanity enjoy health and well-being. God has opened various channels to enable this to happen. The different medical systems that people pursue should be understood within the context of God bringing health to all.

An African theology of healing in contexts of HIV requires that scientific progress in the development of antiretroviral drugs be embraced as a miracle that God has worked in the

[123] Henri J. M. Nouven, *The Wounded Healer: Ministry in Contemporary Society*, New York, Image Books, 1979, p. 93.

[124] See V. S. Molobi, 'An African Theology of Healing and Its Impact on HIV and AIDS', *Studia Historiae Ecclesiasticae* 31, 2, 2005, pp. 313–32.

contemporary period. The 'resurrection effect' or 'Lazarus effect' attributed to antiretroviral drugs – enabling human bodies to 'become beautiful' again – demonstrates the power of God. [125] The dichotomy between biomedicine and faith healing tends to restrict the power of God. It creates the misleading impression that researchers work outside God's jurisdiction. If one accepts the theological assumption that all creation is under God, one can appreciate the complimentary nature of healing systems.

The gospel of prosperity and prophetic/charismatic healing in Africa are useful reminders that an inordinately futuristic eschatology may not be satisfactory to many people. They call upon churches to work towards making available abundant life in *life before death*. Heaven must descend on earth. Medication must be provided to all those in need. The proclamation of the good news entails the struggle to ensure that the basic needs of Africans are met. There must be 'a cohering of economics of health and economics of salvation into an integrated economy of life.' [126] When the church in Africa strives towards this ideal, it will realize its capacity as a healing community.

Wounded Healers: The Church as a Healing Community

So far, we have dwelt on claims of physical healing of HIV and AIDS because it is the most controversial dimension. However, churches in Africa have performed other types of healing with little or no controversy. AIDS competent churches in Africa need to appreciate the idea that the church is a healing community:

> It belongs to the very essence of the church – understood as the body of Christ created by the Holy Spirit – to live as a healing community, to recognize and nurture healing charisms and to maintain ministries of healing as visible signs of the presence of the kingdom. [127]

---

[125] Cochrane, 'Of Bodies, Barriers, Boundaries and Bridges', pp. 10–11.

[126] Paul Germond and Sepetla Molapo, 'In Search of Bophelo in a Time of AIDS: Seeking a Coherence of Economics of Health and Economics of Salvation', *Journal of Theology for Southern Africa* 126, 2006, p. 47.

[127] Jesudasan and Ruppell, *Healing as Empowerment*, p. 57.

The churches in Africa need to approach the theme of healing in contexts of HIV with a great deal of humility. They must acknowledge that they are made up of 'wounded healers'. Members of the body of Christ in Africa are aching in different places. The HIV epidemic has drawn attention to the vulnerability of the church. As it expresses its identity as a healing community, the church in Africa must not assume any superiority over any other group of people. For those among us affected by HIV and AIDS, it should reach out with respect and loving compassion. The WCC Study Document *Facing AIDS* elaborates:

> The church, by its very nature as the body of Christ, calls its members to become healing communities. Despite the extent and complexity of the problems raised by HIV/AIDS, the churches can make an effective healing witness towards those affected. The experience of love, acceptance and support within a community where God's love is made manifest can be a powerful healing force. This means that the church should not – as was often the case when AIDS was first recognized within the gay community – exclude, stigmatize and blame persons on the basis of behaviour which many local congregations and churches judge to be unacceptable. [128]

In fulfilling its task as a healing community in the context of HIV and AIDS in Africa, the church must recognize the need to become a welcoming and hospitable church. I have already described the characteristics of a welcoming church. It is one that is aware of the fact it is a church living with HIV. By offering safe and friendly space to people living with or affected by HIV, the church goes a long way in healing persons and relationships.

Hospitality is a key value in African cultures. It is a vital resource in contexts of HIV. African churches must continue to strive towards building caring, receiving, supporting and (therefore) healing communities. By breaking down barriers and accepting people living with or affected by HIV or AIDS, the church extends a healing hand. Hospitality is

---

[128] World Council of Churches, *Facing AIDS: The Challenge, The Churches' Response*, Geneva, World Council of Churches, 1997, p. 77.

not passive but revolutionary. It transforms the one who extends it into an agent for social change.

In *The Wounded Healer*, Henri Nouven, writing before the HIV epidemic, describes the power of hospitality:

> Hospitality is the virtue that allows us to break through the narrowness of our fears and to open our houses to the stranger, with the intuition that salvation comes to us in the form of the tired traveller. Hospitality makes anxious disciples into powerful witnesses, makes suspicious owners into generous givers, and makes closed-minded sectarians into recipients of new ideas and insights. [129]

As a healing community, the church offers love and friendship. It offers a shoulder to cry on for the bereaved. It visits the sick and the lonely. It cares for grandmothers and children who provide care to orphans. It pays fees for the education of orphans. It listens to abused women and children. It takes up the rights of those of us with HIV or AIDS. As a healing community, the church binds wounds and heals memories. It is a 'church of all and for all'.

The church accompanies the dying. As medical fees skyrocket in some countries, many people on their deathbeds are abandoned and lonely. Their families and relatives often do not have the financial resources to be with them in their hour of greatest need. Women from different denominations visit and say prayers. They heal parched souls and infuse a sense of hope. As a healing community, the church is a hoping and helpful community.

'For in this hope we were saved': Hope in Contexts of HIV

Existential despair, hopelessness and pessimism are some of the direct products of HIV and AIDS in Africa. Dead futures. Coffins. Cemeteries rapidly filling up. Wailing. Groaning. Memorial services. All these have become part of the vocabulary of most communities in Sub-Saharan Africa. God, where is your face? Where are you when these

---

[129] Nouven, *The Wounded Healer*, p. 89.

six orphans have to be parcelled out among relatives who live far apart? Where are you when this only-child, now a teacher, slides toward her grave?

> The searing question 'where is God now?' which has troubled our centuries must be answered in the light of Calvary by looking to the people subject to hunger, poverty, oppression of many kinds, war and HIV/AIDS, and – very often in the developing world – to all these together. [130]

The impact of HIV and AIDS on Africa has led to serious questions about the future. African economies, already marginalized in the so-called new world order, are undergoing further turmoil due to the HIV epidemic. 'Desperate and hopeless sights created by the disease are seen everywhere, in families, communities, government establishments and businesses.' [131]

It is in such an environment dominated by uncertainty that African churches must provide hope. The starting point has to be an honest admission that the HIV epidemic has caused untold suffering and death. It often sounds hollow and insincere to proclaim a message of hope in such a context. However, the church has no choice. Its very identity demands that it brings a message of hope. Hope is the very 'stuff' of being church. 'Churches are channels: hope-bearers – even in the midst of the AIDS pandemic.' [132]

Where Christians are supposed to enjoy abundant life (John 10:10), the HIV epidemic has instead produced suffering in abundance. Instead of joyous laughter, cries of anguish dominate the African soundscape. Whereas in the new dispensation there ought to be 'no infant that lives but a few days' (Isaiah 65:20), many parents in Africa continue to mourn such children. While in the new heaven and the

---

[130] Enda McDonagh, 'A Theological Reflection on HIV/AIDS', in Czerny, *AIDS and the African Church*, p. 69.

[131] Bensen Okyere-Manu, 'Hope in a Time of AIDS', *International Congregational Journal* 3, 2, 2003, p. 172.

[132] Christian AIDS Bureau, in S. Pick, *HIV/AIDS Our Greatest Challenge Yet! The Road Ahead for the Church in South Africa*, Wellington, South Africa, Lux Verbi, 2003, p. 11; cited in Olivier, 'Where Does the Christian Stand?', p. 84.

new earth there shall be no mourning nor crying nor pain (Revelation 21:4), tears of mourning, crying and pain flow freely on Africa's face. Desmond Tutu's words, written during the struggle against apartheid, remain relevant to the church's struggle against HIV. For Tutu, 'the Church of God must produce a relevant theology which speaks to this hopelessness and despondency.'[133]

It is very tempting to manufacture cheap hope on a large scale and splash it over anxious communities reeling from the effects of HIV and AIDS in Africa. Faced with such a vicious epidemic, most Africans would readily hold on to such a hope. However, taking such a route undermines the credibility of the church. Christian hope should not seek to side-step the devastation and suffering caused by AIDS. Any theology of hope that wishes to minimize suffering runs the risk of becoming the 'opium of the people'.

> The way to glory evidently leads through suffering: for in spite of all the joy and beauty life has to offer, there is much sorrow, injustice, tragedy and waste. Some of this we can understand as the consequences – for ourselves and for others – of our own acting in the freedom given us by God; some we cannot immediately understand, though we sense that it may belong to a larger pattern of which we now glimpse only a part. But some suffering, sorrow and injustice we cannot understand at all; and we cry out, 'I believe; help my unbelief!' (Mark 9:24).[134]

Hope: A Vital Resource in the Churches' Response

Although the term *hope* has found its way into public discourse in some African contexts,[135] it assumes a specific theological dimension when it is used within Christian circles. Hope is a concept that runs throughout the Bible and has attracted a great deal of theological reflection. Jürgen Moltmann, one of the leading German Protestant theologians of the contemporary period, has been described as 'the

[133] Desmond M. Tutu, *Hope and Suffering: Sermons and Speeches*, Johannesburg, Skotaville Publishers, 1983, p. 26.
[134] WCC, *Facing AIDS*, p. 34.
[135] Olivier, 'Where Does the Christian Stand?' pp. 81–9.

76

theologian of hope'. [136] His book *Theology of Hope* sets out the Christian basis for hope. [137] Hope is not just an abstract concept in the writings of Moltmann. It emerges from his own practical life experiences. In his autobiographical essay, Moltmann begins with the following words:

> When I was young, the hope of Christ saved my life and has ever since filled my living with energies of the divine Spirit and let me welcome every new day with expectant joy in the coming of God. [138]

Moltmann stresses that Christian hope is not an escapist illusion. For him, Christian eschatology has tended to focus on the *end*, instead of appreciating that God's decisive intervention in history is the *beginning*. Moltmann's reading of eschatology and hope is helpful in contexts of HIV in Africa. It assists churches to recognize the need to transform the present. Moltmann writes:

> Expectations of the end are only Christian if they conceive their future horizons out of the remembrance of Christ's death on the cross and the resurrection of the crucified Christ with the dead into the eternal life of the coming glory of God. For Christ's end, too, was and is, after all, his true beginning. Christian hope of the future does not prolong or extrapolate into the future the lines of the past and the present of world history, in order to postulate a good end or, as is more frequently the case, a bad one. Instead, Christian hope perceives in the cross of Christ the anticipation of the end of this world, which is a time of sin, death and evil. This is because – yes, because – in Christ's resurrection, Christian hope recognizes the deliverance from evil that is present in the beginning of the new life and the new creation of all things. In the energies of the Spirit of Christ, we already experience that new beginning here and now, as we are being reborn to a living hope. [139]

[136] Manfred W. Kohl, 'An Encounter with the Theologian of Hope', *International Congregational Journal* 3, 2, 2003, pp. 139–41.

[137] Jürgen Moltmann, *Theology of Hope: On the Ground and the Implications of a Christian Eschatology*, London, SCM Press, 1967.

[138] Jürgen Moltmann, 'In the End is My Beginning: A Hope for Life – A Life for Hope', *International Congregational Journal* 3, 2, 2003, p. 143.

[139] Jürgen Moltmann, 'Hope in a Time of Arrogance and Terror', *International Congregational Journal* 3, 2, 2003, p. 158.

We need to recognize the tension between the 'now' and the 'not yet' in salvation. An unhealthy preoccupation with the world to come can paralyse the church. Moltmann's theology of hope seeks to turn the church's attention away from an intense focus on eschatology. For him, Christian hope lies in anticipating the transformation of the existing world order. Moltmann contends that God promises to 'make all things new' (Revelation 21:5). The hope for humanity and creation lies in God's promise to transform the world. This is the hope that African Christians possess: when God shall make all things new, HIV and AIDS will be relegated to history.

Hope in African contexts of HIV must not be cheap or magical. Neither must it be optimism in religious garments. Christian hope must grapple with the harsh reality of human suffering. In the specific context of HIV, Christian hope must fire and propel churches into action. According to Denise Ackerman, Christian hope is not passive:

> We have to be actively and passionately involved in trying to bring about that for which we hope. This implies hands-on 'doing'. Hope is not an armchair activity. Hope has very little currency if it is just a 'pie in the sky when we die by and by', a trick masquerading as optimism covered with a religious veneer. True Christian hope is tougher, more realistic; it is essential to the life of faith and actively involved in life. Yet it seems as though hope has 'emigrated from the church'. Perhaps this is so because it is too often understood as referring only to the future. Or perhaps it is seen as simply unrealistic. [140]

Hope is another distinctive resource that the church brings to the overall response to the HIV epidemic. Government agencies and NGOs are not required to be ambassadors of hope. In most instances, they are expected to use non-religious approaches. The church is uniquely placed to bring hope to desperate communities. It preaches messages of hope even in those situations that appear to be utterly hope-

---

[140] Denise Ackerman, *After the Locusts: Letters from the Landscape of Faith*, Glosderry, SA, David Phillip, 2003, p. 81. Cited in Olivier, 'Where Does the Christian Stand?' p. 96.

less. Seeing through the eyes of faith, the church stubbornly proclaims that suffering is temporary. The glory that shall be revealed surpasses the suffering of the present (Romans 8:18).

Ackerman mentions that some might regard Christian hope as unrealistic. According to scientific standards of rationality, most forms of Christian hope are childish, a futile effort to escape the suffering of life. It is through human wounds that the gods enter. Christians are not discouraged by such criticisms. Even when the situation seems depressing, they continue to hold on to the hope that the coming dispensation can only be better than the present. In the case of HIV, believers anticipate a world without the epidemic. Hope is the motor behind the church's significant expansion. This hope embraces the 'now' and the 'not yet' dimensions of existence. Christian hope defies worldly diagnosis of what is possible and what is not. Hope has been and remains the lifeblood of the church. It has nourished persecuted Christians. It has motivated despairing volunteers. It has energized those with HIV who might be depressed.

Donald Messer highlights the centrality of hope to the growth of the church:

> What distinguishes the church from many other organizations is its relentless commitment to compassion and its unconditional love for every human being. The Christian church has never accepted common definitions of 'reality'. Had we done so, the apostles never would have left Jerusalem, taking the gospel to six continents. If Christians had been realistic, they never would have sent out missionaries with the intent of conquering hunger, defeating illiteracy, translating the Bible into every language, upgrading the status of women and children in every culture, starting new churches, or challenging every disease on earth. [141]

Hope has driven the church throughout the ages. For Maria Cimperman, who follows William F. Lynch's reflections, hope is tied to the imagination. As communities hope for a

---

[141] Messer, *Breaking the Conspiracy of Silence*, p. 148.

new dispensation, they imagine what it will look like. They also actively work towards the realization of their vision:

> Hope not only gives us the vision, it sanctions and sustains the vision. Christian hope tells us what type of vision we have. Hope is also a prime Christian resource of the imagination. Hope points to the *telos* of Christianity and offers a horizon of our expectations in both tangible and non-tangible ways. Hope is the vision that allows us to reshape our reality in a particular way. Hope imagines what could be and animates the virtues to bring to life what is imagined. [142]

African churches are mediating hope in contexts dominated by suffering and death. They counter the paralysing effects of HIV. In their proclamation of the good news of salvation, they recharge communities and exhort them to hold on. They reinforce the wisdom captured by a poster that reads, 'A camel can survive for seven days without water. A human being cannot survive for a day without hope.' It is hope that sustains most people living with AIDS in the absence of essential drugs. For many, hope is the only resource they possess. As Joseph Estermann has noted, 'Poor people say, "Hope is the last thing one can lose!"' [143] Churches in Africa must do more to ensure that hope increases among those who are on the verge of giving up.

'Accounting for the hope that is in the church': Signatures of God's Mercy

Reflections on hope in contexts of HIV in Africa can easily become abstract, given the theological debates about it. However, Christian hope is also based on interpreting what has already taken place and is currently taking place. There are developments connected to the HIV epidemic that give rise to a lot of hope for African churches. Hope therefore has two dimensions to it. On the one hand, it emerges when the community of faith turns its gaze to the future. It imagines a new heaven and a new earth, where the HIV

---

[142] Cimperman, *When God's People Have HIV/AIDS*, p. 45.

[143] Joseph Estermann, 'Theology of Hope or Hope for Theology?' *Voices from the Third World* 16, 2, 2003, p. 155.

epidemic is no more. On the other hand, the community of believers should be in a position to explain why it continues to have hope. Thus: 'Always be prepared to make a defence to anyone who calls you to account for the hope that is in you' (1 Peter 3:15).

The Ecumenical Association of Third World Theologians (EATWOT) met for its Fifth General Assembly in Ecuador in 2001. The theme of the assembly (inspired by 1 Peter 3:15) was: 'Give an account of the hope that is in you: weaving the threads of our continuing struggles into a tapestry of hope in the twenty-first century.' Elsa Tamez, writing as an EATWOT theologian, maintained that the reason for hope was located in the paradigm of the resurrection. 'We believe that change is possible, even when it seems impossible.'[144] Similarly, the 'Message of Hope' from the Assembly identified signs of hope in the struggles by victims of colonization, women and other oppressed groups. It noted that sustainable spiritualities of hope were also emerging. [145]

In what follows, we will seek to account for the hope that is in the African churches in the era of HIV. Amid the despair caused by the epidemic, there are signposts of hope. In contexts choking with anxiety, rays of hope are shining through. Despite the doom and destruction, one can discern 'signatures of God's mercy' [146] in contexts of HIV in Africa. No matter how small they may appear to those without the eyes of faith, these developments provide a basis for the church's hope.

Home-Based Care

Some African womanist scholars have rightly pointed out that home-based care is effectively women-based care. Other critics describe how African states have reneged on

---

[144] Elsa Tamez, 'Giving an Accounting of the Hope that is in You', *Voices from the Third World* 14, 2, 2001, p. 28.

[145] 'Message of Hope: Statement of the Fifth General Assembly of the EATWOT', *Voices from the Third World* 14, 2, 2001, pp. 38–44.

[146] I am indebted to Ben Gilpin for this phrase. He used it to describe signs of hope in Zimbabwe in 2006, when the Zimbabwean crisis was worsening.

their responsibility to provide quality medical care to their citizens. Why do they abandon those of us with AIDS in our time of need? Is it home-based care, or home-based neglect? How are elderly parents expected to provide quality care without adequate resources?

Despite these weaknesses, home-based care is a vivid demonstration of love. Women's groups in the various denominations across Africa have led the way in providing concrete examples of the mission of the church. While academic theologians scour libraries and hit their laptops in efforts to define mission in contexts of HIV, African women have acted out the meaning of mission. By visiting the sick, cooking for them and comforting the bereaved, African Christian women are enacting the mission of the church. They are a living example of hope in the face of HIV.

Huge amounts of money have been directed towards the struggle against the epidemic, although much more could be released. Global media networks celebrate donations by philanthropists. All this is admirable. However, few have paused to salute the incalculable service rendered by those who provide home-based care. Simply being available to help the bed-ridden individual to turn over is worth more than any amount of money. Hope does not have the dollar sign engraved upon it: it bursts forth from simple acts of love and compassion. Home-based care is indeed a signature of God's mercy. It bears eloquent testimony that the human project is still viable. It brings out the Christian values of love, acceptance and support.[147] It inspires hope. It shatters the walls of separation created by stigma and discrimination. Families and communities surround sick members with love. They act as a source of hope and inspiration to all those who seek to provide effective responses to HIV.

Home-based care is a practical illustration of the impact of resilience in the face of a major challenge. Despite a debilitating shortage of resources,[148] home-based care has emerged as a very useful model. It shows the need for indi-

---

[147] WCC, *Facing AIDS*, p. 93.
[148] Weinreich and Benn, *AIDS: Meeting the Challenge*, p. 77.

viduals and communities to give all they have in order to make a difference. Christian volunteers have demonstrated that money need not be the defining aspect of human life. There is hope that individuals and communities will continue to give their time and resources for others.

The Church's Positive Response to the Call to Action

The church has been described as a 'sleeping giant' in the face of the HIV epidemic but there is growing acceptance that churches in Africa have begun to take decisive steps to make effective responses to the epidemic:

> Drawing upon the numerous examples from the Bible that demonstrate Jesus' compassion and willingness to 'touch' and to 'heal' those in need, Christian values inspire action. And so today, in every country around the world, there are literally millions of Christians working in response to HIV. [149]

The active participation of African churches is a sign of hope. It is the churches that are strategically placed to ensure that resources are deployed effectively. Churches in Africa have captive audiences on days of worship. They are also able to access more people than political parties. There is therefore hope when churches undertake to make a difference in contexts of HIV.

One of the most notable developments is the increasing number of theological training institutions in Africa that have integrated HIV into their programmes. Graduates of these institutions have acquired the necessary skills to approach the epidemic in a sensitive way. Their skills relate to HIV prevention and counselling, as well as theologies of hope. Graduates who possess up-to-date knowledge of the epidemic are a source of hope, well placed to lead in social transformation.

Although the 'great condom debate' flares up once in a while, churches now appear to have realized that their efforts should concentrate on HIV, not on condoms. Gradually, reluctance to discuss human sexuality is also being

---

[149] Lux and Greenaway, *Scaling Up Effective Partnerships*, p. 47.

overcome within the different denominations. Even global bodies like UNAIDS have acknowledged the considerable progress that churches have made in this regard. Purnima Mane, Director of the Department of Policy, Evidence and Partnership at UNAIDS, writes:

> We are inspired by the many churches who work with marginalized populations such as drug users and sex workers and young people as valuable partners in addressing issues of risk and vulnerability, providing education and often have a sound knowledge of how to work with these groups. [150]

Some denominations in Africa now have HIV and AIDS desks. Personnel from such departments do sterling work, including workshops for preachers where they illustrate how to reclaim the pulpit as a valuable resource in the churches' response to HIV. The acceptance of HIV and AIDS programmes by some denominations is a major source of hope. It shows that the church is beginning to take its responsibility seriously.

The increased visibility of the church in the area of HIV is both a result of, and is reflected by, the expansion of ecumenical and denominationally based HIV and AIDS organizations. The launching of the Ecumenical HIV/AIDS Initiative in Africa (EHAIA) by the WCC in 2002 demonstrated the church's commitment to providing an effective response to the epidemic. The African Jesuit AIDS Network (AJAN), Churches United in the Struggle Against HIV and AIDS in Southern and Eastern Africa (CUAHA), the Lutheran Communion in Southern Africa, the Organization of African Instituted Churches (OAICs) and the Nordic–Foccisa cooperation have actively sought to enhance the overall Christian response to HIV and AIDS in Africa.

The church's 'conversion' to the HIV and AIDS cause has contributed to greater openness. Although theological rigidity continues to fuel denial, stigma and discrimination, the participation of the church has gone some way to reduce

---

[150] Purnima Mane, 'Churches in the Lead on HIV Prevention Reinvigoration', *Contact: A Publication of the World Council of Churches* 182, 2006, p. 4.

84

these negativities. The church's contribution to prevention, treatment and care instils a sense of hope. Churches in Africa have begun to respond positively to the invitation issued by the WCC:

> The church is called to stand with persons who are affected by HIV and AIDS. This 'standing with', this service of the church on behalf of those who suffer, will take different forms in each situation depending on the needs and possibilities. In some cases the church will need to work for better medical care for affected persons; in other cases, to work for improved counselling services or for the defence of basic human rights or to ensure that accurate factual information is available within the church and to the general public or to ensure that a climate of understanding and compassion prevails. Most of the time all these efforts and more will be needed. [151]

Networks of Committed Religious Leaders

The leadership of the church has tended to approach the HIV epidemic as an issue for 'those out there' – outside the sacred space occupied by the church. This has fuelled stigma and discrimination. However, the emergence of organizations like the African Network of Religious Leaders Living with or personally affected by HIV and AIDS (ANERELA +) is a source of hope. Founded by the Ugandan Anglican priest, Canon Gideon Byamugisha, ANERELA + shows how the HIV epidemic affects everyone, including those at the top of the religious hierarchy. [152] ANERELA + is a continental network of African religious leaders from diverse religious backgrounds. It was officially launched in October 2003 in Kampala, Uganda. [153]

The courage that members of ANERELA + have shown in disclosing their HIV status is a positive indicator that the

---

[151] WCC, *Facing AIDS*, p. 44.

[152] For a description of ANERELA + 's operations, see Astrid Berner-Roderеda, *HIV and AIDS in Africa: A Female Epidemic Requiring Only a Female Response? The Gender Dimension of HIV and AIDS and Good Practice Examples from Partner Organizations of Bread for the World*, Stuttgart, Bread for the World, 2006, p. 32.

[153] Gideon Byamugisha and Glen Williams, eds, *Positive Voices: Religious Leaders Living with or Personally Affected by HIV and AIDS*, Oxford, Strategies for Hope Trust, 2005, p. 7.

church is making some gains in the struggle against the epidemic. [154] ANERELA + encourages individuals to undergo voluntary testing and counselling in order to establish their HIV status. As religious leaders, their openness has a positive impact on the community of faith's response to HIV and AIDS.

Networks like ANERELA + have helped to promote the Greater/Meaningful Involvement of People with HIV and AIDS (G/MIPA) in the life of the church. This has contributed to the questioning of the 'us' and 'them' attitude that has dominated approaches towards those of us with HIV. Such networks are beacons of hope in the response to HIV.

Advances in Research and Increases in Funding

Hope has also been inspired by the progress made in HIV prevention and treatment. Although no vaccine has yet been discovered, dramatic advances have been made in treatment. Such advances imply that testing HIV positive need no longer be a death sentence. The significant strides that have been made have given a new lease of life to many people who were on their death beds. Although millions of people living with HIV in Africa do not have access to antiretroviral drugs, there remains a real hope that the situation will improve dramatically in the near future. Some African countries (e.g. Botswana, South Africa, Zambia) have begun to provide free antiretroviral drugs to those who need them. This is an empowering sign of hope.

Advances in research have followed from increases in funding. While it is clear that rich countries and corporations could contribute much more than they do, funds released so far are a source of hope. The resources that have been made available by individuals, foundations and governments have lifted up spirits. Given greater commitment by all, HIV should no longer spell doom and destruction.

---

[154] For the testimonies of some of the prominent members of ANERELA +, see Byamugisha and Williams, *Positive Voices*.

Conclusion

The church is an abiding institution with a long record of compassion. In the Bible, it possesses a valuable resource that has nourished communities of faith across generations. The church is regarded as a credible institution with a unique capacity to mobilize volunteers. Its workers are consistently well motivated, while its members have diverse professional backgrounds. All these things mean that the church can provide effective and sustainable responses to one of the worst disasters the world has ever seen.

However, weaknesses remain, including stigma and discrimination, theological rigidity, gender insensitivity, negative attitudes toward sexuality, external dependency, and limited experience in fundraising, monitoring and evaluation. The church in Africa needs to tackle these limitations to ensure that it provides an effective response to HIV.

Perhaps the greatest source of hope in the face of the HIV epidemic is the unbroken African spirit. The epidemic has killed and orphaned millions and left a trail of destruction, yet the African spirit remains unbroken. Africa has survived the horrors of the slave trade and colonialism. It has endured poverty, civil strife, natural disaster and other huge setbacks. The continent's people have shown a remarkable capacity to withstand such crippling experiences. They have faced the HIV epidemic with a resolute spirit.

In a special edition of the *Ottawa Citizen*, the guest editor, Stephen Lewis, the United Nations Special Envoy for HIV/AIDS in Africa, saluted Africa's resilience. He expressed the hope that the pandemic could be beaten, if only the world would support Africa in its quest for survival. He detected signs of hope in the life-saving drugs that are now available. However, his greatest source of hope was not in falling prevalence rates in some parts of Africa. Rather, it was informed by the unbroken African spirit. Lewis' salute to that spirit is profound:

> I have been in the Envoy role in Africa for more than five years, and I do have hope, deep and abiding hope. But it's grounded in a very different set of factors. In the first instance, what most of the western world fail to understand is the range of knowledge, sophistication, solidarity, generosity and sheer, unbridled resil-

ience at the grassroots of the continent, particularly amongst the women. We underestimate Africa; we always underestimate Africa.

The nurses working a 10-hour overnight shift alone in an adult ward with 70 patients, the vast majority admitted with AIDS-related illnesses; the grandmothers, ancient, frail, impoverished, raising 10 or more orphan grandchildren; the volunteer home-based care workers trudging from hut to hut through the village, painstakingly swabbing the skeletal bodies of the near-dead and dying; the counsellors in an AIDS clinic explaining gently, tenderly, to a young mother that she has tested positive and what it means; the support groups of people living with AIDS sustaining each other, finding food for each other, checking on each other with optimism and laughter and love – so much of the continent engaged in the struggle for life, but never, never giving up. We talk glibly of heroism. Africa is its embodiment. [155]

Lewis, a remarkable supporter of Africa's struggle against HIV and AIDS, identifies its unsung heroes. He recognizes that 'big money', celebrities and top researchers are important. However, it is the grandmothers, volunteers and health workers who are quietly but decisively voting for life in the face of death. Drawing inspiration from the conviction that 'we shall overcome', daughters and sons of Africa engage in simple but life-transforming and life-enhancing activities in contexts of HIV.

John Mary Waliggo, a Catholic theologian from Uganda, also believes Africa will overcome the HIV epidemic. He finds comfort in history: Africa has survived malaria, smallpox, sleeping sickness, the slave trade, colonialism, famines, conflicts, wars, genocide and hunger. He is convinced that the optimism expressed by the Catholic Bishops of the African Synod in Rome, 1994, must continue to guide Africa:

Africa will live. Africa will survive. Africa can and will defeat the present challenge of HIV/AIDS. The factors for this strong belief in Africa's optimistic future are: God loves Africa and will never let it be wiped away. Africans have great inner energies and indigenous resources, which when well tapped, can

---

[155] Stephen Lewis, 'A Message from Stephen Lewis', *Ottawa Citizen*, 13 August 2006, 'Hope in the Shadow of AIDS', p. A2.

88

effectively contain, control and eventually fully eliminate the HIV/AIDS threat. Any genuine believer and follower of Jesus Christ has no alternative but to be an optimist. The good, the true, the just will always finally defeat the evil, the untrue and the unjust. [156]

The churches in Africa are empowered to face the HIV epidemic because of their unflinching hope that another world is possible. They press on because of their faith in the promises of God. Their hope is stubborn; it refuses to grant the last word to death. It is hope that is grounded in the belief that the cross and resurrection of Christ represent a new beginning for humanity. This hope must inspire the churches to work towards a better world; one where the HIV epidemic is no longer a threat to life.

> The cross calls for patient surrender but at the same time for protest (lament), the resurrection awakens a sense of victory and empowers one to face suffering. The power of the resurrection, however, does not lead to resignation and passivity. It can even make one rebellious and assist one in one's struggle against suffering. [157]

Churches strive to make a difference in desperate situations because they possess hope that can be termed stubborn. This hope is sustained despite the prevailing HIV scenario. It is inspired by the vision that some time soon, and very soon, the epidemic will be fully contained.

The church's hope also springs from the conviction that there is something in the heavens. Despite the suffering, the church remains certain that the heavens will bring about a new dispensation.

---

[156] John Mary Waliggo, 'Inculturation and the HIV/AIDS Pandemic in the AMECEA Region', *African Ecclesial Review* 47, 4, 2005 and 48, 1, 2006 (AMECEA 15th Plenary: Responding to the Challenges of HIV/AIDS within the AMECEA Region), pp. 297–8. Italics original.

[157] Daniel J. Louw, 'The HIV Pandemic from the Perspective of a *Theologia Ressurectionis*: Resurrection Hope as a Pastoral Critique on the Punishment and Stigma Paradigm', *Journal of Theology for Southern Africa* 126, 2006, p. 111.

Extracts from Mercy Amba Oduyoye's poem *Biribi Wo Soro (There is Something in the Heavens)* provide a fitting way to end this book:

> We know it.
> There is something in the heavens
> God, let it reach us.
> Our hands are stretched out in supplication
> For we know it.
> There is something in the heavens
> God, let it reach us.
> Peace with justice
> Sharing the earth's bounties
> Justice for peace
> People with compassion for the fallen
> We know it.
> God, there is something in the heavens
> Let it reach us.
> We sow the seeds of hope
> We expect a harvest of love
> We sow the seeds of justice
> We expect a harvest of peace
> We sow the seeds of compassion
> We expect a harvest of solidarity
> God, rain upon our efforts
> The rain that transforms is from you.
> We know there is something in the heavens
> God, let it reach our hands.
> Our hope is real. [158]

---

[158] Mercy Amba Oduyoye, 'Biribi Wo Soro', *Voices from the Third World* 14, 2, 2001, pp. 11–12.